The Platform Owner's Guidebook

THE PLATFORM OWNER'S GUIDEBOOK

HOW INDUSTRY EXPERTS UNLOCK VALUE FROM ENTERPRISE SOFTWARE

SHANE WILLIAMS

Published by Shane Williams

First published in 2021 in Melbourne, Australia

Copyright © Shane Williams

www.shanewilliams.com.au

Melbourne, Victoria

This book uses stories to enforce the meaning behind relevant chapters. Permission to use these stories has been provided.

Every effort has been made to trace (and seek permission for use of) the original source of material used within this book. Where the attempt has been unsuccessful, the publisher would be pleased to hear from the author or publisher to rectify any omission.

All inquiries should be made to the author.

Edited by Jenny Magee

Typeset and printed in Australia by BookPOD

ISBN: 978-0-6451617-0-0

ISBN: 978-0-6451617-1-7 (ebook)

For my three sons – I hope having a Dad as an author inspires you in some way to put your ideas out into the world, to give back, and make the world a better place than the one you've inherited.

ACKNOWLEDGEMENTS

This book wouldn't have been possible without the kind contribution of time and expertise shared by the many professionals I interviewed. Your challenge to my thinking and the new and interesting lights you shone on the topics expanded and ultimately enhanced the concepts, ideas and stories. Taural Rhoden, Matt Porter, Rudi Khoury, Jason van Lint, Ben Duncombe, Mike Kasparian, Simon Baldock, Nigel Dalton, Frank Cuiuli, Steve Baines, Rory Fitzpatrick, David Dawson, Fiona Blaufelder, Dominique Franco, Rachel Brennan-Behan, Evy Suwono, Casey Moon-Watton, Glenn Jones, Sophie Gregory and the 'HR Tech Groovers' – Josh Grace-Ware, Jane Seevaratnam and Sambit Das – thank you!

A special thank you to my reviewer Taural Rhoden who persevered through the early drafts, provided invaluable feedback, and undoubtedly improved the flow and congruence of the messages.

I'd also like to acknowledge my mentor Alex Hagan for encouraging me to write the book. Lynne Cazaly for teaching me the superpower of 'ish'. Kate Burke for showing me what's possible. Emma McQueen for her endless positivity, energy and tough questions. My editor, Jenny Magee for transforming my brain farts into something people might read. Sylvie Blair of BookPOD for her publishing wizardry. And my accountability team of Joannah Bernard, Christine Yip, Bob Ratnarajah, Ross LaRosa and Jade Lee for keeping me honest to the word count every day through the process.

A shout out to Mum and Dad. Their sacrifices through the 1980s and early '90s afforded us kids a solid education. I might not be the lawyer you imagined, but hey, an author is ok right?

Most of all, I want to thank my gorgeous wife Kelly for her constant encouragement and understanding. She did all the heavy lifting – including keeping our three boys occupied – that gave me space to write books and chase crazy dreams. Most of all, thanks for putting up with me. Love you.

CONTENTS

Introduction   1

    The platform capability   5

    Characters   12

PART ONE: OPERATIONAL VALUE

Maturity Level One: Implement   17

    Define and protect your culture   19

    Integrate your delivery team   29

    The butterfly effect   35

    Organisational readiness   39

    Executive ownership   45

Maturity Level Two: Rationalise   51

    Platform vision   53

    Managing capacity   61

    Employee value proposition   69

    Leveraging networks   85

    Dogfooding   95

    Finding the right answer   103

    Balancing debt   113

    Keep it simple(r)   121

PART TWO: STRATEGIC VALUE

Maturity Level Three: Realise   131

   Show me the ~~money~~ value   135

   Love the problem, not your solution   143

   Prioritising with data   151

   Platforms are rarely islands   159

   Taking stock   165

   Sustaining high performance   171

Maturity Level Four: Amplify   179

   The pilot's chair   181

   Becoming missionaries   187

   Do the right thing   195

Final thoughts   200

References   202

About the Author   209

INTRODUCTION

Dark clouds are forming as enterprise software becomes increasingly expensive and customers wrestle with the lack of transparency about the ongoing effort and cost required to realise a return on their investment.

Like warships, the big platform players exert their force over the market. The insatiable appetite for revenue growth is an almost unstoppable force. When the 100-year storm hits, the generals proclaim loudly how well their subscription models insulate them from the fallout, and their customers are left to weather the storm alone.

Salespeople patrol the waters like whaling ships disguised as research vessels, seeking highly prized targets with a model that prioritises selling product over delivering value. The value equation is weighted too heavily in favour of the vendors. As soon as you're dragged aboard, you're committed (long-term) to more resources than you need with a strict no-returns policy.

Implementation partners also navigate the waters – although until they've boarded, it's often unclear whether they are peacekeeping soldiers or unscrupulous pirates. You might be saved from sinking, but there's every chance you'll have a musket stuck in your chest before you realise your ship is taking on water.

In many organisations, the job of navigating the waters and safely charting a course falls to one individual – the platform owner. A seasoned captain who understands the trade routes is a master negotiator and leader. Those platform owners who've been in the game a while often get the opportunity to captain a number of these ships and, along the way, meet a vast number of fellow captains to share rum and tall tales.

But I'll let you in on an industry secret that nobody wants to talk about. Like Captain Jack Sparrow from the Pirates of the Caribbean, the art of being captain lies largely in folklore and luck. We're all trying to figure it out.

Chances are you picked up this book because you're looking for a silver bullet? You're an executive seeking ROI who knows something needs to change in your organisation, or maybe you are the platform owner desperately looking for a lifeline.

> Chances are you picked up this book because you're looking for a silver bullet?

Sound familiar? I get it; I've been there. Can I hazard a guess where your head is at?

You have stakeholders lining up with an increasing list of expectations and timelines. Perhaps you're wondering if you have the right team or even what the right team looks like. There's a good chance the vendors are knocking down your door, and you want to look like you know what you're doing lest they take advantage of you. Perhaps the implementation project just kicked off, and you're worried it's going to get away from you. Or maybe the implementation is long since complete, and you're landed with an organisational ugly duckling – with the expectation that you'll fix it.

Do you want to know how I guessed? It's because most execs and just about every platform owner I've ever met says the same things.

There's good news, though. These platform investments don't have to be an unmanageable, increasing expense. Sure, there's an ecosystem of vendors and partners keen to get their hands on your money, but thousands of organisations get tremendous value from these platforms. They're the case studies you read about.

There is also a growing number of platform owners who've weathered the storm before you. Some of those people are now the most successful platform owners in the world. They've become EVPs in their organisations who speak at international conferences about the value delivered from their platforms. You'll find their stories (and not just the successes) contained within these pages.

In this book, you'll learn about the four levels of platform maturity and how to navigate the 'must-dos' to progress through the levels. You'll learn the techniques used by the pros to get stakeholders on board, drive adoption, build high performing teams, and deliver exceptional value.

Why did I write this book? Well, after making my share of mistakes, I've learned a lesson or two. And now that I work with inspiring organisations across the world, I've decided there's no reason why you should live with the same pain or make the same mistakes. It must be costing organisations billions; money that would be better spent on creating improved products or solving social inequality.

This book is my way to give back to my peers. It is the book I wish I'd had when I started my journey. I had been working in technology for fifteen years before being thrown into platform ownership. As a technology executive in a massive, global, media organisation, I thought

> As a technology executive in a massive, global, media organisation, I thought I had it all figured out but quickly learned I knew two-fifths of f**k all.

I had it all figured out but quickly learned I knew two-fifths of f**k all. Now I am out the other side, and having had the opportunity to share experiences with numerous veterans, I want to pay it forward so you can leverage the more than ninety combined years of platform ownership wisdom in these stories to unlock and inspire your journey.

That said, if you're looking for a blueprint, you won't find it here. If your platform ownership journey was a holiday, this would be a guidebook rather than an itinerary. While every journey is unique, this book focuses on what not to miss. It will help you avoid your predecessors' mistakes and share lessons from those who did well and those who screwed up.

> While every journey is unique, this book focuses on what not to miss.

So, grab yourself a notepad and pen, or perhaps a highlighter, and let's kick off your journey.

THE PLATFORM CAPABILITY

FLYING SPIDERS

Hong Kong is a fascinating city; with a unique blend of east meets west. One of the best parts of my trips to China is not the food, history or architecture (which are all amazing) but something far more mundane; bamboo scaffolding.

In building construction, scaffolding is erected around a structure to elevate workers and materials and provide a level of support and protection during the construction process.

While it seems most of China now prefers steel or aluminium, Hong Kong remains a stronghold for the practice of bamboo scaffold construction with more than 1,700 registered bamboo scaffolders known locally as 飛天蜘蛛 or 'flying spiders'. In many respects, using bamboo makes sense as China is home to forty per cent of all known bamboo species. Bamboo has a higher tensile strength than steel, is lighter, faster to construct, cheap, sustainable and likely far safer than steel if affected by a typhoon.

Much like a high-rise in Wan Chai, an enterprise software platform can't be built without concepts such as architecture, foundations, engineers, processes and safety. Following this analogy, if your platform is to be a high-rise, then the team, processes, and governance you build around it are scaffolding. I call this a **'capability'**.

WHY A CAPABILITY?

In her PhD thesis, Dr Cecily Macdougall, CPA, estimated that only 64 per cent of software projects in Australia succeed, with $5.6B wasted annually on projects that either don't deliver benefits or are abandoned (Walker, 2016). I'm sure you'll agree that's not a positive statistic. There's a raft of reasons for this – a quick Google search for 'why technology projects fail' returns 217 million results. Writing in Forbes magazine, Bernard Marr reckoned that 54 per cent of failures result from mismanagement – as opposed to three per cent for technology problems (Marr, 2016). Therein, I think, lies the case for a capability. Too many organisations fall into the trap of buying software to solve problems without realising that success comes from what you put in place to leverage the software effectively.

> Too many organisations fall into the trap of buying software to solve problems without realising that success comes from what you put in place to leverage the software effectively.

THE PLATFORM CAPABILITY MODEL

Having worked with several global organisations and met a vast array of platform owners across many industries and geographies, I developed the below platform capability model to articulate the components required for sustainably amplifying value from platform investments.

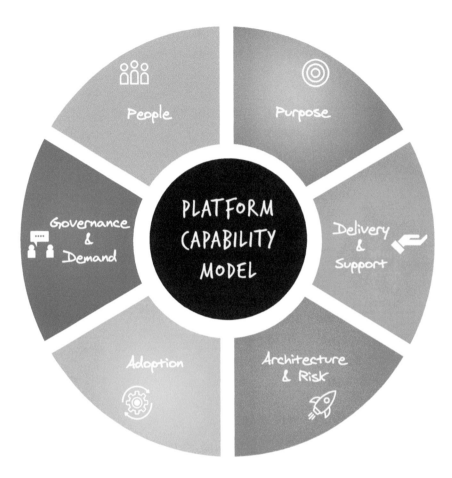

The model comprises six domains: Purpose, People, Governance & Demand, Delivery & Support, Architecture & Risk, and Adoption. More than sixty competencies sit behind these domains, against which the capability can be measured to ensure the platform investment is fully optimised.

Let's explore each domain in a little more depth.

Purpose means creating a clearly defined and easily articulated connection between business objectives and platform strategy. You want everyone across the organisation – from the executives, through sales, service and marketing to your technical team – to be able to articulate what strategic business imperative is being targeted and how platform investments and business process transformation will achieve that imperative.

The **People** domain is about creating a strategy to attract and retain top talent, ensuring systems are in place to foster innovation and being deliberate about learning and career progression. This is critical because it is difficult to attract and retain top talent, yet the ability to best leverage the value of the platform lies in retaining the unique IP of your organisation and your implementation.

Governance & Demand is about ensuring robust assessments of ongoing platform investments with executive commitment aligned to the realisation of expected benefits. It is critical in ensuring investments made in the platform achieve material bottom-line results, including prioritisation and buy-in from business stakeholders. Not only does this build belief in the value, but it also creates accountability with your internal customers.

Delivery & Support refers to the ways of working and measures by which the delivery teams will design and deliver solutions. It is, in essence, defining how the engine will operate and finely tuning that engine for optimal performance.

Adoption is far more than change management. While training and communications are essential foundations for enabling your stakeholder teams, adoption goes beyond the initial launch to ensure everyone using the platform is adopting the new ways of working and deriving maximum value from the investment.

Architecture & Risk ensure security, privacy and integration are considered, and technical debt is managed. There is a defined enterprise, data and solution architecture with a supporting roadmap that ensures solutions deliver end-to-end.

CAPABILITY MATURITY MODEL

Of course, even if every organisation used this model, not all capabilities would be equal. From my experience and working with platform owners across the globe, I surmise there are four levels of platform capability maturity.

Maturity	$ROI	Effort : Return
Amplify	x 10	1 : 20
Realise	x 5	1 : 10
Tipping Point		
Rationalise	x 1	1 : 1
Implement	x 0.5	2 : 1

(Left axis: upper two rows — Strategic Value; lower two rows — Operational Value)

The model above illustrates the four levels of capability maturity. The first two levels deliver operational value. The investment might be seen as a strategic initiative, and that should certainly be the goal, but when you're starting and delivering dollar for dollar ROI, you can hardly argue you've achieved strategic value. The goal is to get above the tipping point as soon as practical and take the investment to deliver strategic value.

Let's break down the levels:

During the first stage of platform **implementation**, much energy goes into setting up the project and project team, getting delivery underway. There's a hive of change management activity and inevitably a go-live. Typically all of this happens to a predetermined schedule and budget, and the first deployment serves its purpose.

But it's not always a fantastic experience on day one. Plenty of compromises and sacrifices need to be picked up when the project is complete. There is no return on the investment at this stage, and a great deal of effort goes into keeping things moving. As a platform owner, you'll be finding your feet, navigating platform, project, partner and vendor politics. It's a tough gig but getting your hands dirty to build a solid foundation is worth doing.

Once the platform is live, the dust needs to settle. During the **rationalise** stage, the platform team will be busy cleaning up after the project team and establishing how they will work together. Meanwhile, the platform users are dealing with the fallout and learning their new ways of working. Inevitably there's a steady stream of enhancement requests and questions about why specific capabilities were not delivered with the implementation.

As this stage draws to a close, the platform is beginning to deliver value equivalent to cost, and the amount of effort required to run it is stabilising. Most importantly, as a platform owner, you'll now have a team of people around you who have bought into the vision you've set and are ready to go on the journey with you. Similarly, you'll have strong relationships forming with some senior people in your organisation, and the effort equation is equalising – you're destined for great things.

Then you pass the tipping point.

Once the capability reaches level three, we begin to **realise** some strategic value. The capability is beginning to deliver unimagined new value. New relationships are forged within and outside the organisation, and the ideas and experiences of other customers and partners are leveraged to provide exceptional value.

Now, the business sees up to five times the return on its investment, and the return for effort is increasing exponentially. Importantly, you're becoming a driving force in the organisation – a key player who consistently delivers value to the business. You have a team of true professionals behind you and a strong sense of vision and purpose.

If the capability reaches level four, the resulting **amplification** is a total game-changer. The capability delivers real strategic value, influencing the business strategy directly and unlocking possibilities for new markets and business models. The capability model permeates throughout the organisation and unilaterally lifts the capability maturity across all platforms, led by the initial platform capability team. It is likely you have transcended the platform and are leading parts of the organisation.

When we overlay the maturity model on the capability model, it looks something like this:

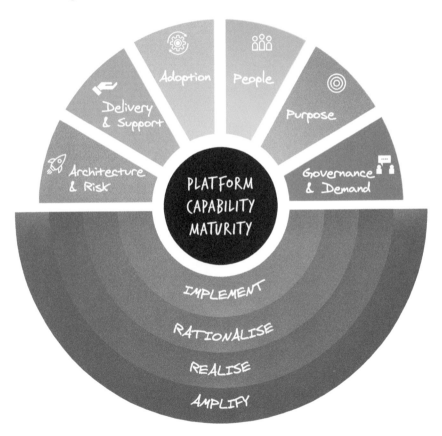

The key to success as a platform owner is to champion and grow the capability and deliver, maintain, and continuously improve the platform. In essence, like Hong Kong's 'flying spiders', you need to build a sustainable, resilient, flexible, supporting structure around your software, then progressively mature that to amplify value for the organisation.

As we journey through the book, the platform capability maturity model will show which dimension and maturity level we're discussing.

Now that you understand the capability and maturity models, let's dive in and learn what it takes to get you and your platform capability from good to great.

CHARACTERS

Before we begin, I want to introduce you to our protagonists. To protect the confidentiality of those who contributed true stories, I've developed three recurring characters through whom we will live the platform journey.

Jennifer, Lucas and Deepika are platform owners beginning their journeys on different platforms in different organisations at varying maturity levels.

'What the hell have I just got myself into?' says Jennifer, a career technology professional.

The CIO has just spent 25 minutes pumping up Jennifer's tyres about the fantastic job she's done over the last few years leading two massive transformation projects for a global media company. Somewhat caught up in her self-importance and fuelled by the flattery that's coming thick and fast, Jennifer misses the cue that this isn't an ask; she's been 'voluntold'. Her new role is to take ownership of the advertising systems portfolio. With nobody in the current position, Jennifer is immediately accountable for all advertising booking and provisioning for the Australian businesses.

'Just don't f**k it up', adds the CIO.

≈

Down the road is a global financial services company that, eighteen months ago, decided to pilot a new HRIS platform for its small business sales and marketing teams. Lucas was a lead in the HR team of their Australian arm for six years and played a key subject matter expert role in the pilot. Today Lucas has been summonsed, along with his manager, to the APAC CEO's office.

'Lucas, we've been really impressed with the success of the implementation here, largely due to your input and influence', opens the CEO. 'How would you like to move to the US for a few years and lead the global transformation across EMEA and North America?'

≈

Meanwhile, in a tech hub east of Melbourne, the technology team that provides technical support and manages the ITSM tooling in a national retail chain has just been introduced to their new leader, Deepika. While she has been with the team for some time, this is her first day in the role. Their ITSM tool is relatively mature, having been implemented some three years earlier, and Deepika is excited by the challenge and opportunity to bring real value to the organisation.

The internal all-staff CEO memo reads 'Deepika consistently demonstrates an unwavering focus on customer outcomes, and her passion for people and professional development is integrally aligned to our organisational values. We are exceptionally excited to be able to create this opportunity for one of our own people and trust you'll all join us in celebrating Deepika's appointment to this newly created position.'

PART ONE
OPERATIONAL VALUE

Maturity	$ROI	Effort : Return
Strategic Value ↑		
Amplify	× 10	1 : 20
Realise	× 5	1 : 10
═══════ Tipping Point ═══════		
Operational Value ↑		
Rationalise	× 1	1 : 1
Implement	× 0.5	2 : 1

1

MATURITY LEVEL ONE

IMPLEMENT

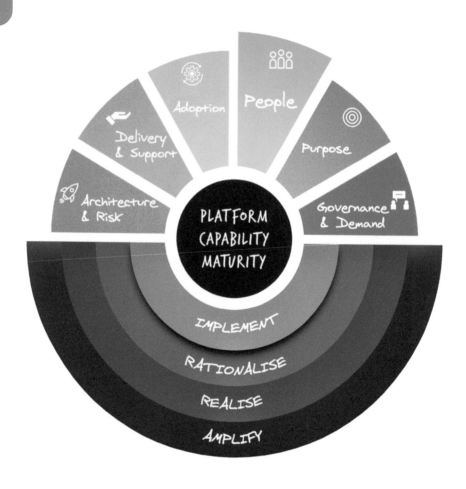

DEFINE AND PROTECT YOUR CULTURE

Lucas landed in NYC in the early summer. Central Park was buzzing, and the forty-minute walk each day from Greenwich Village to the office in midtown was fascinating.

Everyone was keen to meet the new Aussie guy. Did he have a pet koala, did every Australian drink excessively and swear profusely, and were there really venomous snakes and spiders in every house?

By late fall, the glitter had worn off. The daily walk to midtown was replaced with ride-shares, and the loud office banter, particularly with the technology crew, had turned into quiet acknowledgement. By this stage, the implementation partners had rolled in, and the shirt-and-tie cubicle workers were not impressed by those in t-shirts and jeans standing around whiteboards with Post-It notes. These people insisted on non-standard hardware, weren't attending the change advisory board and kept pushing back on the standard project reporting.

Lucas had a lot on his plate. He knew this was how you implemented software, and if he ran a traditional IT shop, he'd never attract the right talent to join his team. But at the same time, Lucas needed the support of the tech organisation to be successful. How would he forge a new path within the boundaries of the existing norms?

WHEN STRATEGY AND CULTURE COLLIDE

'Culture eats strategy for breakfast' is a well-known adage, often attributed to the late management consultant and author Peter Drucker.

There is much wisdom in this statement and plenty of research and anecdote to back it up. But platforms are rarely introduced to maintain the status quo. More often than not, a transformation agenda underpins the desire for an organisation to invest significant sums of money into new platforms. This is despite the genuine desire to maintain the company culture that is espoused as a competitive advantage. Some executives don't consciously realise the oxymoron of transformation and preserving culture, while others seek to quell the noise of their real agenda with disingenuous rhetoric about the value of the existing culture. Even if they genuinely want to maintain the majority of the culture but 'grow up a little', a strategic objective that requires transformation is at odds with the status quo, and the platform owner is often the face of that change.

WHY WORRY ABOUT IT?

In a 2018 HBR spotlight series on culture, the writers assert that culture is essential to sustainable competitive advantage but can be a significant liability if misaligned with strategy (Groysberg, et al., 2018).

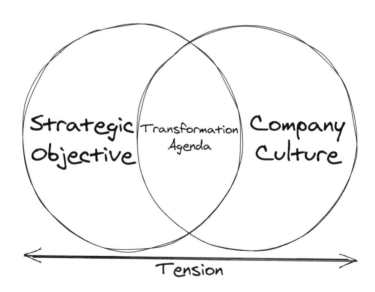

If I were drawing this on a whiteboard it would look something like this.

With that in mind, lets pause and consider the situation. You're about to implement a new platform that will impact the lives of numerous stakeholders. A CRM might have a significant impact on sales and service. A marketing platform on Sales and Marketing. An HRIS on People and Culture and the leadership team, or an ERP on the Finance and Distribution teams.

Then factor in that you're about to embark on a journey that will impact your organisation's technology function.

Are they a technology business? A custom software development shop that will despise everything that comes with a platform saying 'we could build that capability in a couple of months?'

Or perhaps a traditional IT function that understands infrastructure and operations but isn't going to understand how agile teams work and will have no concept of continuous delivery. 'Where is your project plan?', 'Raise a change request', 'That needs to go through the architecture advisory board', 'Log a ticket'.

Every group wants benefits without change, and in the middle of this, you need to build your delivery team to execute the strategy.

> Every group wants benefits without change, and in the middle of this, you need to build your delivery team to execute the strategy.

Welcome to the journey of the platform owner.

How will you take the best of what is good about the organisation that will help you win the support of those you'll rely on and bring something new to the table that will make a difference? Will you be a peacemaker or a game-changer? And how will you get shit done while everyone's on the journey?

CULTURES WITHIN CULTURES

Subcultures exist within every organised society. In his book, *Subcultures*, Ross Haenfler uses music inspired subcultures as examples. The 1960s and '70s brought hippies and discos whose drug culture and free-love would surely be society's downfall. In the 1980s, they gave way to gangster rap and rock music. Gangsters graffitied and had an unhealthy disdain for police, while rock was all about sex and drugs. Hair metal bands challenged conventional gender norms with men wearing make-up and teasing their hair while the heavy metal types were clearly out to bring devil worship to the mainstream. And then came the '90s... you get the idea (Haenfler, 2013).

What is important here is that over time, people in these subcultures had their own unique identity and forged a path that significantly impacted society. They changed the game, then as they became accepted, subcultures were less controversial and more mainstream. (Let's be grateful we don't all have perms.)

What does this have to do with platform investments, you might ask? Well, did you ever have a mysterious new kid arrive at your school who spoke and acted a little differently? I recall that each time someone new joined our school, we were never sure if they were cool or not. They were indeed different and intriguing, but were they rebels, and should we follow or assimilate them?

Given that it's your responsibility to deliver this change to the organisation, consider yourself that new kid. How do you set yourself up for success when you are charged with disrupting the culture that is seen as a competitive advantage and is the reason many people join and stay with the organisation? I think the answer lies in the subculture.

CREATE YOUR SUBCULTURE

Ok, so it might seem fairly bold to embark on creating a subculture in an organisation, but hear me out. This isn't a new concept, as subcultures already exist in every organisation. The classic example is executive management. Harrison Miller Trice described them in his book *Occupational Subcultures in the Workplace* as 'the quintessential bureaucratic work group in our society', who believe they should decide things such as how work should be divided and who should control the selection and training of employees (Trice, 1993). So if we modify the previous model, the opportunity lies in the centre.

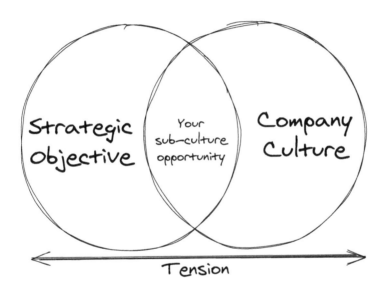

To do this, you'll want your team to establish their values and norms collaboratively. What makes them unique? What is their identity? Why would a new member want to join? What attributes and attitudes

Your subculture should exist to provide an identity to your people that gives them the autonomy to operate within the conventional norms of the organisation but rebelliously challenges the status quo.

To do this, you'll want your team to establish their values and norms collaboratively. What makes them unique? What is their identity? Why would a new member want to join? What attributes and attitudes would new members have that would make them a great fit? How will this new subculture forge its path and gradually take the organisation on a transformation journey? Importantly, how will they hold each other accountable?

With these questions answered, you can establish a team charter and begin to live your new values. Importantly, these become the foundation of your recruitment strategy – for both partner and permanent resources.

Cultural fit will be essential for new recruits. As they weren't involved in establishing the team values, they'll need to be culturally aligned to be a valuable contributing member of the new subculture. Before anyone is hired, have them pass a cultural interview with various team members. During the April 2021 episode of my *Platform Diaries* podcast, Rory Fitzpatrick, from ServiceNow implementation partner CloudGo, told me, 'Hire for culture first' (Williams, 2021). In the platform game, cultural fit is more important than technical fit – you can, and will, train the latter.

> A word of caution. Always remember that your subculture is just that – a culture within a culture.

A word of caution. Always remember that your subculture is just that – a culture within a culture. You'll come unstuck relatively quickly if you attempt to create a counter-culture because successful transformation requires you to make friends and influence people. You aren't here just to build a platform.

THE PAYOFF

This approach can be controversial but is often necessary to effect change in an organisation. Leveraging the rebellious streak can force other parts of the organisation to take notice.

Let's take a look at some well-known organisations for inspiration.

In an article in the Japan Times, Tim Romero shared the story of the rebel subculture that changed IBM in the 1960s. Back then, software engineering was very different from today. Any software shipped with a bug was considered defective, and customers wouldn't pay for such products. It's a very different world today where we've come to expect and accept updates as par for the course. In the '60s, customer expectations meant testing was paramount. The testing team within IBM became a formidable force within the organisation, and engineers often feared them because of their passion for setting out to break software – not just test it. They wore black t-shirts in a culture of dark suits and ties, and they were bold. 'Black Team' members constantly challenged themselves to be better and brighter than the engineers.

Interestingly, many engineers aspired to membership of the Black Team and attempted to win favour with them by improving their code. The subculture lifted both its capability and the broader engineering community by setting high benchmarks. In doing so, it attracted talent to its ranks (Romero, 2002).

> Interestingly, many engineers aspired to membership of the Black Team and attempted to win favour with them by improving their code.

More recent is the Australian success story REA Group – owners of the online real estate advertising portal realestate.com.au. Their share price rose from 99c to $40 over fifteen years, mainly utilising custom-developed software. In 2014 their technology strategy changed to focus their software engineering teams on consumer products that provided genuine competitive advantage rather than being stretched to maintain commodity capabilities. This meant introducing off-the-shelf platforms for finance, sales and marketing. The engineering community was initially outraged, and the platform teams had to earn their place. However, over the following seven years, the platform teams became part of the engineering organisational fabric, and REA's share price skyrocketed to more than $150.

> The engineering community was initially outraged, and the platform teams had to earn their place.

With a few of Lucas's key permanent hires in place, it was time to decide what the team members stood for and who they wanted to be. What vision would they rally around to enable them to push through the tough times ahead, and what values would they live by to keep themselves on track? Importantly, what types of people did they want to attract to the team, and how would they gauge their cultural fit?

Lucas's team spent two days off-site sharing ideas and principles, debating the various vision and value statements. They landed on one key word – challenge. They would be the rebels who would challenge the organisational status quo, challenge the partner to act in the organisation's best interest, and, most importantly, challenge each other. Their vision and values underpinned their successful implementation. Their values were critical to their hiring strategy. Having the right people and ethos allowed them to be *transformational yet drive adoption within the organisation, define the best processes for delivering and supporting their solution, and work productively with their partner. They fitted into the organisation by creating a sub-culture of their own. Along the journey, their peers and stakeholders understood their intentions and worked alongside them. They weren't a threat, just a little different, and that was ok.*

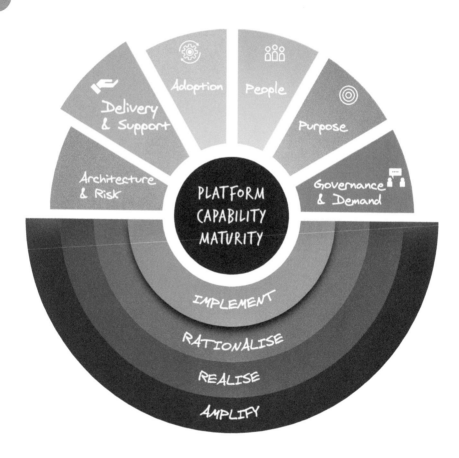

INTEGRATE YOUR DELIVERY TEAM

Jennifer has a tough meeting ahead of her this afternoon. Nobody expects an ongoing multi-million dollar per year running cost; in fact, the business case said we would spend less on people after the implementation. Three weeks from go-live, the project's implementation phase is in its third year and is tipped to clock over the $70,000,000 mark. Not bad for a $35,000,000, eighteen-month programme. Although Jennifer knew recruiting her team was important, it just never seemed more important than all the other urgent challenges that arise daily during implementation – until now.

Jennifer's system implementation partner has kindly put together a road map of work for the next twelve months, including the backlog of descoped requirements, the remediation work that always follows the first go-live and the teams and skills required to deliver that on top of support day-to-day. Jennifer has a million questions on her mind. How will I justify the spend? Will the implementation be successful if we don't have these people? If everyone involved in the project walks out the door, who's going to have the IP? Even if I recruit them tomorrow, who will train my new team? Do I have any commercial leverage with the partner, considering they hold all the cards?

SUCCESS STARTS WITH PRE-SEASON TRAINING

You can be excused for thinking that your platform implementation is a bit like a 100-metre sprint. After all, there's generally a clear finish line, and it's not too far into the future. However, in this analogy, you're facing a marathon, and your implementation phase is little more than pre-season training. By the time the system goes live, you've only just earned your spot on the starting line, and the race is yet to start.

A lot happens during pre-season training. Fundamental decisions about strategy and tactics that will ultimately determine the success of your marathon campaign are made in the early stages. Therefore, it is vitally important to consider how soon you want to take ownership of those decisions and how quickly to mobilise your team so they can be part of the journey.

> The two key ingredients to launching your implementation quickly are capacity and capability.

The two key ingredients to launching your implementation quickly are capacity and capability. In an ideal world, you would start with a fully-fledged team of experienced people in your platform capability, ready to take on the challenge of implementing your platform investment. However, the reality is that few, if any, businesses have the luxury of six to twelve months to stand up a team before kicking off implementation. And that is why often, if not always, implementation partners are engaged. It makes perfect sense when you consider that you want to bring experience to the table and deliver results as soon as possible. Partners have the experience, processes and capacity that you need to hit the ground running.

There is, however, a trap for young players, who focus heavily on implementing the solution and forget the importance of building platform capability.

THE PERIL OF PARTNER-LED IMPLEMENTATION

Implementation partners and the people who work for them are generally well-intentioned, professional people with integrity. They bring a raft of experience and capacity to the table that would take you months to build and recruit. But there are a couple of inherent challenges in many implementations that place tension on the partner. Both are caused by the client and are hard to mitigate.

The first is short-termism – decisions that serve the requirement to hit a date in what is often a fixed-term fixed-price engagement. Under such a constraint, project teams inevitably make decisions that meet the requirements on time and serve the purposes of delivering the project. But if there is no challenging voice from someone who will ultimately own and be accountable for the future ramifications, then such decisions go unchecked.

The second challenge with an entirely partner-led implementation is dependency. It is all too easy (but unfortunately not uncommon) for clients to near the end of an implementation, only to realise they are ill-equipped to take ownership and support of that platform moving forward. Not only do they lack the requisite people capacity, but they also lack knowledge of how the system has been implemented, what decisions were made and why, and what skeletons are in the closet. The client quickly realises they have little choice but to engage the vendor for an extended period to run and support the platform – at a significantly higher cost than running an internal team.

Neither of these is really the partner's fault, but nor are they incentivised to solve them.

Start building your team on Day One – be match fit before go-live.

There is really only one sensible solution to avoid unchecked decisions and vendor dependency after go-live, and that's why it's critical to get things right upfront. The platform owner must ensure that the team members who

> The goal is to ensure the internal team is established and match fit once the initial implementation engagement is complete.

will own and support the system are recruited and embedded in the implementation team as soon as possible after deciding to implement the platform. The goal is to ensure the internal team is established and match fit once the initial implementation engagement is complete.

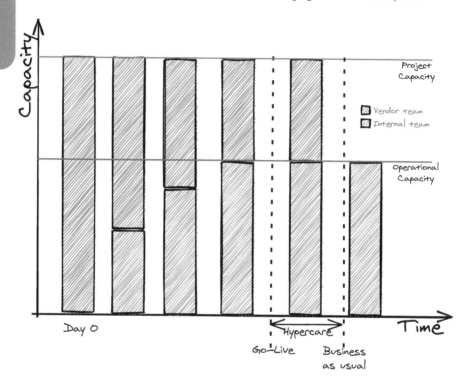

The model above (which we'll build on in Maturity Level Two) illustrates the process of building out the internal team and ramping down dependency on the partner. This enables you to build your internal capability as your team is involved in the build and decisions. It keeps your vendor honest in challenging short-term decisions and ensures you aren't left with a perceived gun to your head for expensive ongoing support. Instead, you'll have a strong partnership that will provide ongoing value to both organisations.

PRO-TIP

Challenge your partner to get you match-fit. Partners bring delivery processes, document templates and established ways of working that enable continuous delivery. Moreover, their people are often highly motivated by the opportunity to coach and mentor. Upskilling from the partner team and adopting the established ways of working are great ways to ensure you can continue to deliver value once the platform is in. The partner value extends well beyond getting your software live, so make the most of the engagement.

Jennifer's executive stakeholders were less than impressed. The business case was already strained, and the exec had no appetite to absorb major ongoing costs. Unfortunately, the impact of the change on the organisation was so significant that they could ill afford any ongoing support challenges. Having no internal team to assume ownership left them no choice. To minimise the bottom-line impact, the executive opted to recontract with the partner for a skeleton crew. This, however, resulted in significant delays in the remediation of bugs delivered during the program and allowed no capacity for delivery of the backlog of descoped items. As a result, the business struggled with adoption and thus its return on investment.

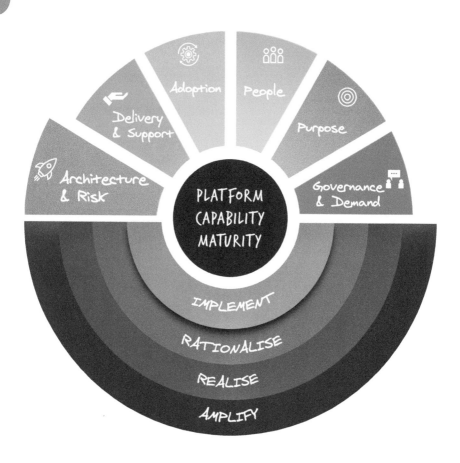

THE BUTTERFLY EFFECT

'For want of a nail, the shoe was lost,
For want of a shoe, the horse was lost,
For want of a horse, the rider was lost,
For want of a rider, the battle was lost,
For want of a battle, the kingdom was lost,
And all for want of a horseshoe-nail.'

– Benjamin Franklin

If you've not seen the 2004 sci-fi thriller with Aston Kutcher, I won't spoil it for you – but I do recommend you watch it (The Butterfly Effect, 2004). The title comes from an idea within chaos theory that the flap of a butterfly's wings can produce a typhoon half a world away. With all software, custom or purchased, there are often limitations or obstacles that result from past decisions. The industry refers to those challenges as technical debt (which we'll cover in more depth in Maturity Level Two). For now, remember that decisions made early in your platform implementation can have lasting effects into the future, so it's critical to think and tread carefully when you are starting.

> Just to make life difficult, there's an essential nuance with off-the-shelf platforms where, unlike custom software, some decisions are irreversible – regardless of how much engineering effort you apply.

WELDING DOORS SHUT

Just to make life difficult, there's an essential nuance with off-the-shelf platforms where, unlike custom software, some decisions are irreversible – regardless of how much engineering effort you apply. I once worked with a project manager named Steve, who used the phrase, 'leave the cables hanging out the back', meaning that a solution should be designed and implemented to allow further expansion or reversal if found to be suboptimal. While that philosophy applies most of the time in SaaS platforms, there are instances where once you walk through a door, you weld it shut behind you and can never go back.

Thankfully there aren't many of these, but they do exist and are generally made during initial implementation, making this one of the most crucial aspects of platform ownership to get right at Maturity Level One.

DON'T LEAVE THE APPRENTICE UNSUPERVISED WITH A WELDER

The best way to deal with this problem is to make it clear to your team, from the beginning, that any irreversible decisions need an exceptional level of critical debate. Define a standard method for documenting the options, costs and consequences for these decisions. One option should always be to debate how you would solve the same problem if you chose not to make the irreversible platform decision. If you don't have a specialist architect on your team, bring in one from your integration partner. Once everything is understood and debated (using a customer and technical lens), ensure the arguments and decisions are clearly documented. I guarantee you'll be referring back to it.

> The best way to deal with this problem is to make it clear to your team, from the beginning, that any irreversible decisions need an exceptional level of critical debate.

COSTLY DECISIONS

A well-known manufacturer has been wrestling with its CRM platform implementation for almost a decade. They've achieved some remarkable results from their investment, and the vendor uses them as a global customer success story. But an early irreversible decision on how to recognise both individuals and companies as customers continually causes challenges for the platform team when innovating new capabilities. They estimate some features involve up to 30 per cent additional development effort to work around the challenges arising from a simple decision made a decade ago.

> Early irreversible decision on how to recognise both individuals and companies as customers continually causes challenges for the platform team when innovating new capabilities.

REFLECTION QUESTIONS

Will you be using any functionality that requires an irreversible decision? Do you have a framework to deal with those decisions?

Have you thoroughly considered your data model? Every organisation is different.

Has every integration and integration pattern been significantly challenged to ensure fit for purpose?

Do you have an experienced architect available to make recommendations?

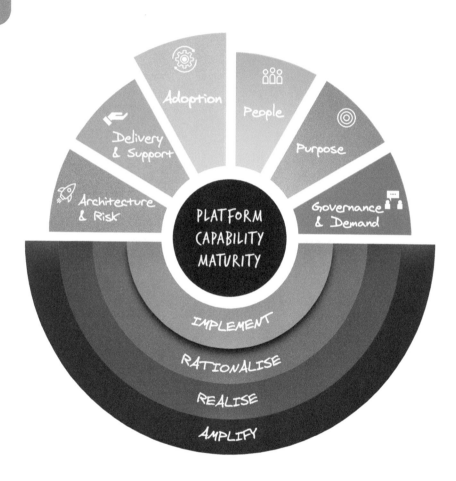

ORGANISATIONAL READINESS

'We can't keep building widgets; we need to start changing behaviour. We've proved the software is fit for purpose because the other contact centres are going gangbusters. Why don't we ask our best performer how they're using the system and get the team to learn from their example?' With those famous last words, Jennifer had unwittingly taken the bait – hook, line and sinker.

The Brisbane team was lagging significantly behind the rest of the country in adopting the new platform. A week earlier, Jennifer had chaired the program's executive update meeting and presented figures showing how well the program was going. The CEO was a particularly analytical chap who immediately honed in on a detail Jennifer was hoping would be overlooked – adoption in the northeast region. After an embarrassingly unconvincing excuse from the regional VP, the CEO tasked Jennifer with visiting the Brisbane team to 'sort it out'.

'Great idea Jennifer!' smirked the regional VP, who was still secretly reeling from the embarrassment of being called out in front of the CEO the previous week. 'Meet Scotty, our top performer. Scott consistently exceeds his targets month after month; he's the top salesperson for three years running. I love Jennifer's suggestion of having our top performer set the example for the team. So Scotty, can you please share with Jennifer and the rest of the team how you use the new CRM system.' Scotty grew up in Logan (a notoriously tough neighbourhood) and had used his natural charm combined with fearlessness to work his way to the top. He owned a huge house in the exclusive suburb of Bulimba and was the envy of most of the northeast sales team – a classic rags to riches story. He had that team in the palm of his hand, including the RVP.

Scott stood up and picked up a small moleskin book. He held it high in the air and turned around to make sure he was the centre of attention. Looking Jennifer squarely in the eye, he proclaimed loudly, 'Here's my CRM!' and slammed the book on the table in a manoeuvre reminiscent of a SuperBowl touchdown.

A raucous cheer erupted, and Jennifer knew she had no friends here.

ADOPTION IS MORE THAN CHANGE MANAGEMENT

If you've been through change programs, you'll be aware of critical roles like change champions (or evangelical early adopters), concepts like Jeff Hiatt's ADKAR, and the Kubler-Ross change curve (the valley of despair is forever etched in my memory).

While all of those principles are useful, fighting the resistance that gets traction in adopting enterprise platforms is a game of push and pull.

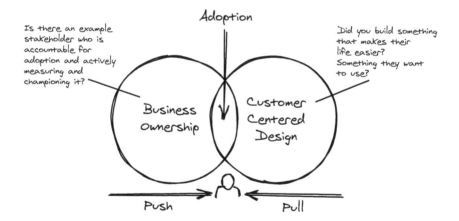

For the more visual amongst us, the diagram above is an attempt to explain this concept. To get people to adopt a new technology requires two key ingredients; software that's as good or better than its predecessor and an executive sponsor who actively supports the business change. After all, technology change should support the business change, not be the reason for it.

SUPPORTING TRANSFORMATION REQUIRES MORE THAN WORDS

Do you ever see those social media posts 'supporting' a great social cause? Have you ever 'supported' one with a 'like'? It's easy to do when it takes little to no effort. Executives will generally genuinely support a transformation initiative and speak proudly and confidently about it. However, while they support it, the change typically has little or no impact on their day-to-day. After all, the chief commercial officer likely has a team of analysts and management accountants providing bespoke customised reports. The origin of the data on which reports are based may change, but it will still be packaged in the same way. For them, the change involves seeing numbers move in a particular direction. This uninvolved support is the same as your social 'like' – it achieves very little. That's not to say you don't need the organisational figureheads talking the talk – you certainly do – but you'll get far more traction when they walk the walk.

EASY LIKE A SUNDAY MORNING

I love coffee and camping. Every visit to the camping store sees me pick up something I didn't set out to buy. Now, if you're anything like me, you've probably picked up something from a store that kinda does the job, but it's too hard to use. One of my more recent purchases was a device that allows you to use Nespresso coffee pods while camping. It does what it says on the box; you put a pod in one compartment, boiling water in another, screw it all together and pump a handle on one end to produce enough pressure to push the boiling water through the pod and into your cup. The result is a reasonably good shot of espresso. I've used it once and gone back to coffee bags. Why? Well, partly because I'm not entirely convinced that putting boiling water under extreme pressure, in my hands, hundreds of kilometres from a hospital, is a great idea; but mainly, it's just way too much effort compared to the coffee bag.

Can you imagine being asked to fundamentally change the way you work supported by a system that does the job but provides marginal benefit, is harder to use, or you simply don't trust? Platform teams do this all the time; then wonder why people fail to adopt.

BUILD IT (AS GOOD OR BETTER), AND THEY WILL COME (WITH ENCOURAGEMENT)

Changing a habit is hard – ask any smoker or fad dieter. The best chance of success comes when you create the perfect storm. In a health sense, that might be a significant health event coupled with the realisation of mortality and a desire to 'be there for the kids'. Sometimes referred to as carrot and stick, simultaneous positive and consequential motivators work a treat.

I've tried lots of different carrots, with Top Ten leader-boards and awards playing to ego and the competitive nature of people, financial incentives and any number of other combinations. Most only have a moderate impact. On the flip side, I was once told of a Bottom Ten laggard-board that shamed those who didn't adopt. I'll spare the guilty the embarrassment of being named.

After a decade of trying different approaches and talking to hundreds of people trying to tackle the same challenge, I've landed on something that, so far, has never failed.

1. Build something valuable, and

2. Engage the executive stakeholder.

And this brings us back to push and pull. The push is your executive stakeholder actively engaging with and using your platform to drive behavioural change. The pull is the unquestionably 'must have' feature or automation that your new platform delivers better than what was available before. Something that I want to use that helps me get over the loss of my comfort zone.

Jennifer returned to Sydney, deflated and somewhat bemused. Since the northeast team had all the same technology and resources as their interstate counterparts, Jennifer knew the adoption solution wasn't technical in nature. She ensured that all the RVPs got a heightened level of service for the next month, with lots of support, webinars and their reporting needs given priority. At the subsequent executive program update, Jennifer outlined how the RVP had supported her suggestion to make Scotty the region's change agent and lead the team by example and how her platform team had delivered significantly more support than usual to give the RVP the best chance of success. The other RVPs chimed in about how supported they felt. The CEO was both excited and concerned. As one of their top performers, the CEO knew Scott well. If Scott was on board, this should be a walk in the park – yet early indicators suggested there'd been no change.

Two weeks later, the Northern RVP moved into the special projects team, and a new RVP who was a staunch supporter of the new CRM was promoted and relocated from Melbourne. Melissa had also grown up in a tough neighbourhood and made her way to the top. She ran a tight ship – 'If it's not in the CRM, it doesn't exist'. It took Scotty about eight weeks to realise the power of the new tools, firstly by being forced to use them, then gradually realising the efficiencies he could get from automation. Sure, it was a little more laborious than writing in his moleskin, but his pipeline reporting wrote itself and the effort required to bring proposals to clients halved. Scotty wanted more and became the biggest advocate in the country. Nationally, adoption increased exponentially as each region attempted to outdo the other. Revenue grew ten per cent as everyone jumped on board, wanting to emulate Scotty's success.

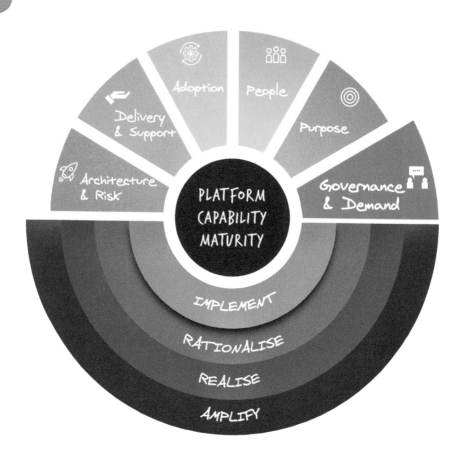

EXECUTIVE OWNERSHIP

'Luc, we need to have a chat'. Lucas's boss was an older guy who'd been around the block a number of times. He seldom looked concerned, but today his face told a different story.

'I want you to know I have your back on this one, but I need to give you some tough news,' he continued. Lucas's mind was racing; this was all a bit out of left field.

'You've lost the support of the sales leadership team; the chief commercial officer has just had a meeting with my boss and asked that we take some corrective action.'

Lucas was bewildered and angry; did corrective action mean sending him and his family back to Australia? Why were the sales leadership turning on him?

'Adoption hasn't improved, and it's starting to slow down in other places. The CCO has taken on the feedback of his leadership team. They say you've stopped listening to them, and the capabilities they need to make the project a success haven't been prioritised. They're concerned that you've become combative and stressed rather than collaborative.'

Some of the more influential people in the leadership group had been resisting the change for a while. It was easier to blame the system for not having the next widget than to adopt new ways of working. And it was a lot easier to throw Lucas under the bus than making any significant change.

'I want you to take a couple of weeks vacation to decompress, and we'll work out how to fix this when you get back,' he concluded.

It was clear to Lucas that now wasn't the time for debate, so he reluctantly took his vacation. His family enjoyed a trip to Florida.

On his return, something unexpected happened, and it was a game-changer.

NAVIGATING THE STORM

Even if you've never watched the 1960s television show *Gilligan's Island,* you're probably familiar with it from pop culture. A group of people from different walks of life set off on a three-hour boat tour from Honolulu. Their vessel, the SS Minnow, is no match for a tropical cyclone, and they are shipwrecked on an island in the Pacific Ocean (Gilligan's Island, 1964-1967).

As a platform owner, kicking off an implementation can be like a tiny ship venturing into the vast Pacific Ocean in a cyclone. You'll most likely be hammered from all sides and faced with having to make constant course corrections if you want to avoid being beached, or worse still, get yourself scuttled.

> The key to navigating significant platform investments has many people rolling their eyes – it's governance.

The key to navigating significant platform investments has many people rolling their eyes – it's governance. The decisions, tradeoffs, and, importantly, the driving force of transformation stems from good governance.

HAPPY INVESTORS AND POWERFUL ALLIES

There are hundreds of decisions to make during a transformation project. We've already discussed many of the fundamental ones, such as how you build your team, how you deliver and support critical architectural choices, and determining the most useful features for your stakeholders. Many of these decisions need organisational guidance, investment and support to be successful. Setting up the best governance frameworks will be critical to your success. Getting governance right limits the likelihood or impact of rogue stakeholders and serves to ensure you own and constantly course-correct the narrative about value and investment with your executive team. The last thing you want is investor fatigue.

Friends in high places

In high school, there were two types of kids you didn't mess with. The bullies who had (or convinced you they had) some form of martial arts training, and the kids with older brothers also at the school. The former group you largely avoided or attempted to keep happy, but the latter were far more influential. They could go about bending social constructs and behaviours to their liking without needing to command and control because everyone knew, even the bullies, that there was potential for consequences if they stepped out of line.

A platform owner typically enters the playground as either an existing popular kid or an interesting new kid. That works for a little while, but popularity is fickle and easily eroded, and new and interesting lasts all of the first week. The big brother kid has far more chance of success in the long haul because those who consider resisting (or those game enough to try it) will soon be re-educated by the big brother. So, to be a successful platform owner, I strongly advise you to find a big brother – an active executive sponsor.

> A platform owner typically enters the playground as either an existing popular kid or an interesting new kid.

While the executive sponsor's role is critical to success, they need to be actively engaged in the program to be effective. That means providing more than passive support. They need to be demonstrating the change and leading from the front. Simply being an influential name that you can throw around or a powerful face at a few town halls isn't enough. Consider the senior manager who doesn't want to change – there might be more than 100 people in their sphere who will not adopt new ways of working if they don't. But as soon as their boss starts asking regular pointed questions about why certain metrics aren't reflected in the platform, their behaviour quickly changes; and because when numbers roll up, those 100+ people suddenly have an incentive to change.

> Your executive stakeholder must also hold sufficient gravitas with their peers…

Your executive stakeholder must also hold sufficient gravitas with their peers; after all, platform investments, more often than not, touch multiple parts of the organisation, so you'll need them to be able to compel their peers to course correct in their patch and lead their teams with a similar level of active involvement and stewardship.

CHECKING THE PULSE

In their 2017 *Pulse of the Profession* paper, the Project Management Institute found that 77 per cent of projects at champion organisations have an engaged executive sponsor who uses their position and detailed knowledge of how the project relates to business strategy to remove roadblocks, make quick and effective decisions, and influence executive leadership (Project Management Institute, 2017). So, unless you're the CEO or senior enough in the organisation to compel change, the industry numbers say good governance, including a solid relationship with your executive, supported by an engaged executive 'big brother', provides a significantly better chance of success.

Before Lucas had time to fire up his laptop, his mobile phone rang.

'Hi Luc, it's Joe,' it was the CCO who'd set off the alarm bells initiating his sudden holiday.

'I'm going out to grab a coffee. Have you got time to join me?'

Lucas wasn't sure what to think, as coffee with Joe wasn't a common occurrence, but he headed out to the front of the building to meet him.

Joe set about understanding Lucas's perspective on how things were playing out before his break and making sure Lucas understood the views of the Sales leadership.

'I can see why making adoption of the platform your responsibility is flawed, and I don't think we've set you up for success, Luc. I'll own that, and I apologise. From this meeting forward, I am your executive sponsor, and I am taking accountability for this organisation getting value from the platform. That said, to fix this, I'll need you to lean back in, and I'll make certain my leaders need to do the same. One team, one dream. Are you in?'

Maturity	$ROI	Effort : Return
Amplify	x 10	1 : 20
Realise	x 5	1 : 10

Strategic Value ↑

========= Tipping Point =========

Operational Value ↑

Rationalise	x 1	1 : 1
Implement	x 0.5	2 : 1

MATURITY LEVEL TWO
RATIONALISE

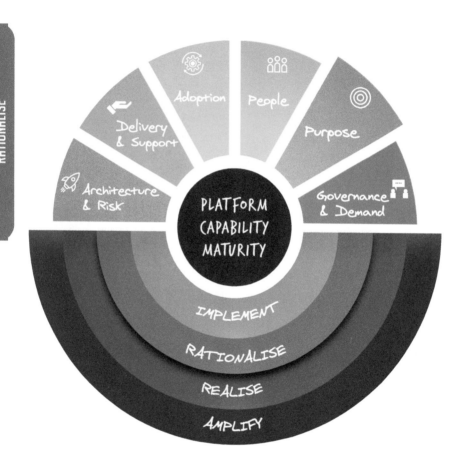

Adoption

People

Delivery
& Support

Purpose

Architecture
& Risk

Governance
& Demand

PLATFORM
CAPABILITY
MATURITY

IMPLEMENT

RATIONALISE

REALISE

AMPLIFY

PLATFORM VISION

Lucas's team was glad the dust had settled on the go-live of the project, but was still really busy with a lot of cleanup work to do.

While the team was transitioning out of project mode and working through its new operational ways of working, team members started to ask, 'What now?' It wasn't about a lack of work, rather a lack of purpose. Where were they headed, and how would their work add value to the organisation into the future?

Lucas, on the other hand, had time to think about this during his break. As soon as the team had some breathing room, he was ready with a plan.

PURPOSE

THE PLATFORM IS IN... SO NOW WHAT?

Welcome to Maturity Level Two. Hopefully, your implementation phase wasn't too painful, and the dust is starting to settle. I bet you thought it was tough, or at least exhausting, but here is where the rubber hits the road.

This stage is all about stabilisation and building your new ways of working to enable future innovation and scale. But you don't want to get stuck here. You've got a little wiggle room after go-live, but stakeholders quickly lose patience if you can't deliver the promised benefits of speed and agility, and you risk spinning wheels and never moving to Level Three if you're not already thinking about where to go next.

Honestly, this part of the journey is going to hurt. It's like those first few weeks at the gym where you're pushing hard on the treadmill for little return. You can't afford to rush it, or you'll injure yourself and delay moving past the tipping point. Likewise, you really don't want to be here longer than necessary.

To get where you're going, you need to know where that is.

Until now, the purpose of the program and your team was set in stone – get the platform deployed. Now it becomes a little murkier. What is your purpose?

At Level Two, that answer is relatively simple,

1. Cleanup the mess from Level One
2. Stabilise and find your operating rhythm
3. Define your purpose.

Yep, your purpose is to find your purpose; while you keep the lights on and set yourself up for success.

WHAT IS PURPOSE AND WHY SHOULD YOU CARE?

I believe purpose lies at the intersection of Vision and Values.

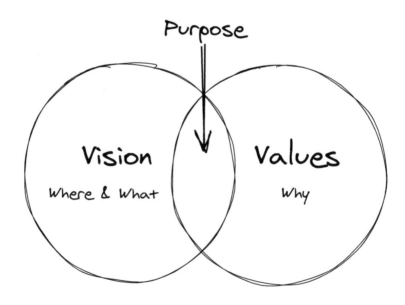

When you know where you're headed, what success looks like and, importantly, why you're doing it, you achieve a sense of purpose.

The first part of a purpose is vision. Where are you taking your team and the organisation? What does the future look like when you've been successful? How has the organisation changed for the better, and how has your team contributed to that? This isn't a plan. The team will work out the plan, and, frankly, having a plan without a vision is pointless. When you inevitably make mistakes along the road, a vision will allow your team to re-orient and get back on track. To quote boxing legend Mike Tyson, 'Everyone has a plan until they get punched in the mouth.'

> When you inevitably make mistakes along the road, a vision will allow your team to re-orient and get back on track.

The second part of the purpose equation is values – finding the why. Simon Sinek is famous for his work on how great leaders inspire action by starting with why. He proposes that people won't truly buy into a product, service, movement, or idea until they understand the why behind it (Sinek, 2011).

But how does this why relate to your platform team? In his book *Extreme Ownership*, Jocko Willink recalls the story of his Navy Seal team heading into a dangerous mission in Iraq. Willink was instructed to take the local, ill-equipped Iraqi soldiers with them. Willink considered this a significant risk to his team and anticipated pushback. When he questioned the move, he was told that the intent was to train these soldiers so that the Seals could eventually leave the combat zone. With that knowledge in hand, he explained to his team why the risk was warranted, and the mission went ahead without incident (Willink, 2018).

Understanding your team's why is also critical for hiring decisions, closely linked to culture from Level One. Alignment of personal and group values provides a smooth transition into the team for new hires and is vital in maintaining team morale when pressure builds.

As I said, Level Two is tough, so you want to keep a close eye on morale. Absenteeism is a key lead indicator of declining mood, whereas presenteeism is good for business. The PWC 2002 Global Human Capital Survey Report found a strong correlation between absenteeism and profit margin (Voisey, et al., 2002).

LEADERS PROVIDE DIRECTION, NOT DIRECTIONS

So how do we turn purpose into momentum and results? Once you've established your purpose, it's time to provide the team with direction. If we were to extend the previous model, then direction would wrap the purpose something like this:

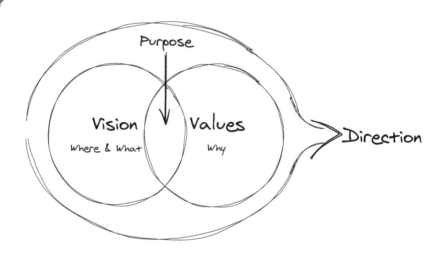

For the sake of absolute clarity, direction is the why, where and what. If you've got the right team in place, they'll be better placed to tell you the how. I believe the difference between a leader and a manager lies in this subtle distinction; a leader doesn't need to dictate the how. Let's break it down further.

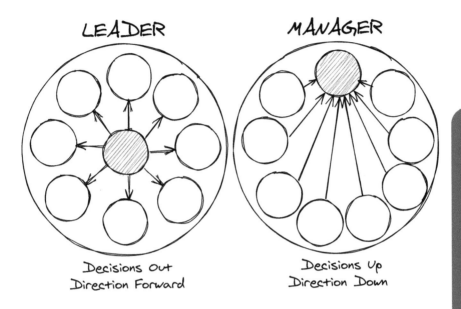

The differential here is that the manager has a team of dependents. Decisions are brought to the manager, and directions about executing are passed down.

Conversely, the leader has a largely autonomous team. They push decisions to the point closest to the outcome, where an intimate understanding of the context ensures the best decision.

My advice is to push through Level Two as quickly as possible. Be a leader and provide direction rather than directions.

> My advice is to push through Level Two as quickly as possible. Be a leader and provide direction rather than directions.

SURELY WE COULD JUST EXECUTE WITHOUT ALL THIS PURPOSE MALARKY?

So far, we've covered the need for purpose and autonomy in your team. Still not convinced? Let's explore the alternative. As you can see in the model below, a haphazard approach leads to either limited output or unhappy teams.

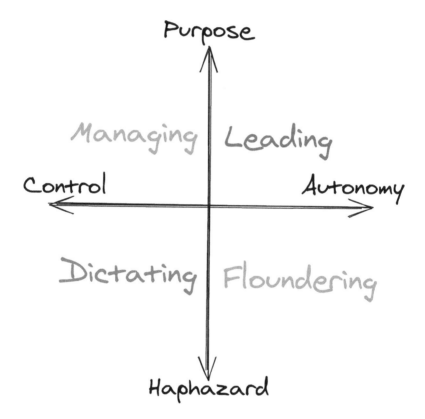

Teams that have the autonomy to make decisions but lack direction spin their wheels, working through their backlog without much enthusiasm. In return, the organisation receives little value. Stakeholders quickly lose faith and interest, and if your team survives, it never escapes Level Two.

The collision between a lack of purpose and a controlling manager is terrible news for everyone. This style tends to produce a dysfunctional team plagued by absenteeism and turnover.

Throughout the project, Lucas had learned plenty about the challenges of the North American HR team and was fascinated by the similarities to Australia. In particular, attracting and retaining talent was an ongoing issue, and Learning and Development capability was spread across many trainers in pockets of the business.

Lucas ran a full-day offsite and took his team through his observations of the organisation and where he saw immense opportunities. The organisation had lots of products, lots of salespeople, and lots of technologists. But it struggled with making sure everyone was up to date with the latest information and training that mattered for their roles. Moreover, competitors were attracting their best talent because their employer brand wasn't the hottest ticket in town. Lucas envisioned a transformation of learning and development; to create an organisation-wide, world-class learning culture that armed salespeople with the best product information. That would translate into more sales and an employee value proposition that attracted talent because it invested heavily in their learning and career development.

This was a vision the team could get behind, and they knew they were sitting on the HRIS platform that would unlock that potential.

'Get this thing stable as quick as you can, team. As soon as I get the leadership across the line on the vision, we'll have plenty to do'. The team had its direction.

PURPOSE

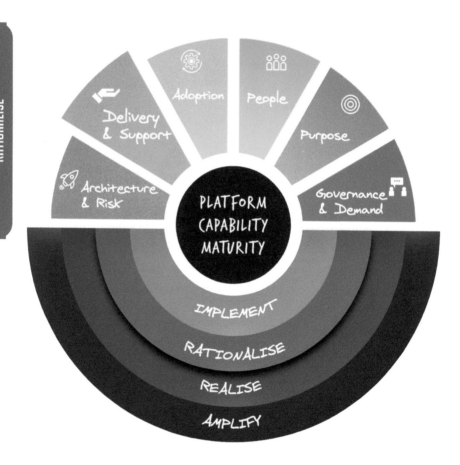

Delivery & Support

Adoption

People

Purpose

Architecture & Risk

PLATFORM CAPABILITY MATURITY

Governance & Demand

IMPLEMENT

RATIONALISE

REALISE

AMPLIFY

MANAGING CAPACITY

'How do you get so many projects done with a team that size?' asked a CIO from a competing bank.

Lucas had never considered that his team was achieving more than anyone else. To him, they were constantly re-prioritising and turning down work. Lucas had just spoken at a tech conference in San Francisco, and there was a line of people keen to pick his brain after the short but punchy presentation.

'I can only justify a half dozen roles. Then each time we have a new request, we have to go through the capital approval cycle and essentially start again. And don't get me started non-project blowouts,' added the CIO.

ACTION AND REACTION

You're likely familiar with the scenario; a project takes longer than anticipated, costs blow out, or things stakeholders initially said were needed end up missing or replaced with others. It's the age-old time-cost-scope conundrum where movement in one has an impact on the others, in a three-way tug-of-war.

> Lucas had never considered that his team was achieving more than anyone else. To him, they were constantly re-prioritising and turning down work

As each project arises, you're asked to predict what will happen several years into the future (when you consider annual budget cycles, etc.).

> The market and business itself have evolved; there are new ideas and people involved. The whole thing is a moving feast.

When the time comes, the appropriate budget year arrives, you go through the approval process and money is released. You spin up a team, perhaps buy some hardware and software and get to work. The market and business itself have evolved; there are new ideas and people involved. The whole thing is a moving feast.

Fixed-price, fixed-scope – that's the answer, right? Find some sucker willing to realise your dream with such constraints. You can, and many do. But you either get exactly what you asked for (which isn't necessarily what you need) or a bunch of change requests each time you realise you need something different, which is essentially scope impacting time and or cost.

FINDING CERTAINTY IN UNCERTAINTY

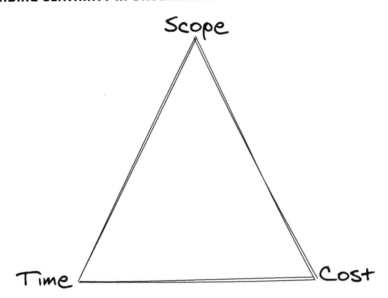

What am I getting at? Let's reflect on the age-old project triangle above. In this scenario, nothing is certain. To achieve 'what you need' rather than 'what you think you need', scope always changes. No matter how expensive your crystal ball or what methodologies you put around them, time and cost flex accordingly. This makes investing in platforms difficult. So how about we make it easier to invest?

CFOs like certainty on time and cost, and when you explain it, everyone understands the scope dilemma, so let's not fight it.

If scope change is a given, what if we could provide certainty and confidence in two of three dimensions to those investing?

> CFOs like certainty on time and cost, and when you explain it, everyone understands the scope dilemma, so let's not fight it.

STARTING FROM SCRATCH

Once you've understood your purpose and tied your team's roadmap to the business goals and objectives, it's time to figure out what the optimal team looks like.

> The principles of zero-based design work well for organisational design in a platform team.

The principles of zero-based design work well for organisational design in a platform team. I suggest adapting the zero-based org design work of McKinsey, the idea being to start with a blank sheet of paper and build the necessary team from the ground up based on three principles (Onno Boer, 2018).

1. Keep the lights on. This represents the amount of people capacity and skills needed to keep your business from falling over, but no more. Imagine you were retiring the platform and just needed enough people to keep it running until you turned it off – no enhancements, no improvements, no reporting – just break-fix.

2. Optimal Capacity. This is the team you need to deliver the business objectives and key results. Think of it as all the people you need to continually improve the platform to meet the business needs, launch new products, maintain existing capabilities. You might forecast this number to grow or shrink throughout the year if you add or remove capabilities from the platform. But operational capacity should represent the team size and skills critical to delivering the business objectives.

3. Project or Flex Capacity. This represents the larger, transformational short-term projects. To deliver a significant step-change in capability (such as implementing a new

MATURITY LEVEL TWO
RATIONALISE

recruitment portal on your HRIS platform). This project might require more temporary capacity or new skills to deliver to the project timeframe and train the operational team. That doesn't mean the team isn't involved in the project, but without the temporary capacity or resource, the initiative wouldn't be successful or might not meet the required timeline.

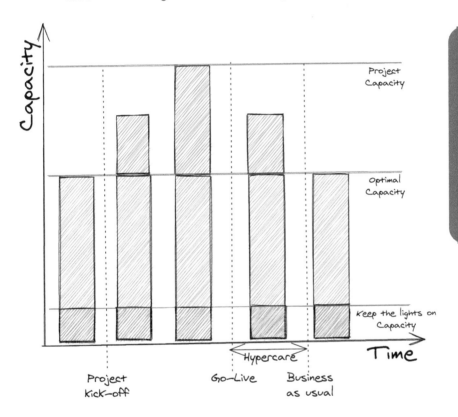

DELIVERY AND SUPPORT

Let's revisit our capacity model. The sweet spot is to get agreement from the executive on the required spend to achieve the strategic objectives of the business and lock in the optimal capacity for the year.

You'll note in the diagram above that the starting point before project kick-off, and the endpoint position after hypercare are the

> It's all about ensuring that the organisation gets predictability in costs.

same optimal capacity. There may be occasions when this lands slightly higher after the initiative owing to an increase in operational maintenance; strictly speaking, this would constitute an increase in 'keeping the lights on'. Such ongoing capacity requirements should be negotiated and agreed upon before the work kicks off. It's all about ensuring that the organisation gets predictability in costs.

PROVIDING CONFIDENCE

Once you've locked in the capacity to deliver on the business objectives with the optimal team, you can then offer the executive certainty on cost and provide some assurance that the people, IP, and ways of working will remain relatively consistent and predictable throughout the year. Notwithstanding churn, this will allow for greater certainty with time estimates when sizing work and thus achieve fixed time and cost goals. At this point, delivery becomes a constant game of prioritising (and re-prioritising) scope to fit within time and cost. With its burst flexibility, this model also allows the business to deliver on tactical projects that come about to combat market forces. It also enables delivery on those occasional projects from a particular line of business or department that want to self-fund something over and above your committed capacity. All this while not derailing your other commitments – think M&A activity which you may not be privy to during planning and budgeting.

Case studies by McKinsey & Company found that organisations could be up to 50 per cent more efficient by using zero-based org design principles, reducing costs and increasing agility (Onno Boer, 2018).

Lucas had rarely seen the issue the CIO had described and was fascinated. The two committed to continuing their conversation after returning from the conference. Over subsequent months, it became apparent that both organisations ran similar strategic planning and set clear objectives and measures for success. However, when it came to mobilising teams, the CIO had a small group of admins and relied entirely on contingent labour for his enhancement work. Moreover, his budget process meant every initiative had to be individually justified and funded, with frequent delays in the approval process. Unpredictability in the availability of resources, time to ramp them up and limited ability to retain IP meant both continuous improvement and projects took longer and were more costly. Time, Cost and Scope were always fluid.

On the other hand, Lucas's efficiency came from having consistency and certainty on capacity and capability. He had a similar level of demand but didn't have to worry about funding approval delays, ramping people up and down, or associated knowledge transfer. His costs and times were fixed, and he spent most of his time ruthlessly prioritising (managing scope).

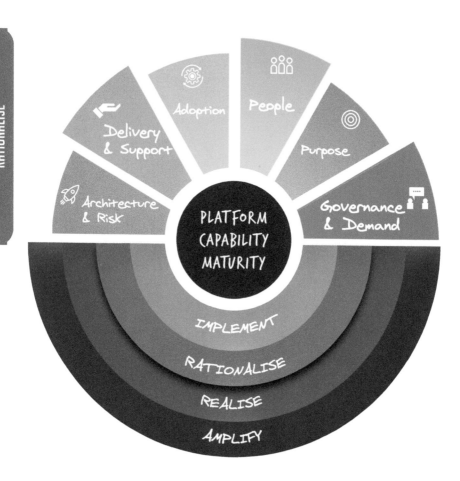

PLATFORM CAPABILITY MATURITY

People

Purpose

Governance & Demand

Adoption

Delivery & Support

Architecture & Risk

IMPLEMENT

RATIONALISE

REALISE

AMPLIFY

EMPLOYEE VALUE PROPOSITION

WHY WOULD THEY WANT TO WORK FOR YOU?

When looking for or attempting to retain talent, most leaders focus primarily on the fantastic opportunity they're providing; the working environment, employee benefits, and the type of experience that the candidate needs. While useful, it's not the complete picture. Individual motivation is often overlooked in terms of the kind of work enjoyed and how long people like to stay in one organisation.

FINDING THE RIGHT FIT

Understanding these additional dynamics and hiring the best fit for your organisation's forward investment is critical to building the right team. For example, you might find a specialist who ticks all the experience boxes, but your needs go deeper than that. Perhaps you're looking for a technical anchor for your capability, someone who will remain a constant for many years and around whom the team can establish and grow. Your expert specialist is not the best fit because while they have all the experience, it is built and maintained by taking on many short-term engagements. They are driven by the breadth of problems to solve and different technologies to explore. They're less concerned about company values or building a high performing team. Analogously, a brain surgeon is more than qualified to perform general practice, but if you're recruiting a local GP, do you need a brain surgeon, and how would you attract and retain them?

MOTIVATION AND MOBILITY

To understand how to attract and retain talent, let's peel the problem back to basics.

There are essentially two dimensions through which we need to look at this challenge: the type of work the individual prefers and how long they stay with one organisation.

Dimension one (motivation) describes the type of work preferred, from business as usual and steady, continuous improvement (a workhorse) through to fast-paced, high-pressure, short-term work (a racehorse).

Dimension two (mobility) describes the likelihood that the individual will seek new opportunities, from not at all (a stayer) almost certainly (a player).

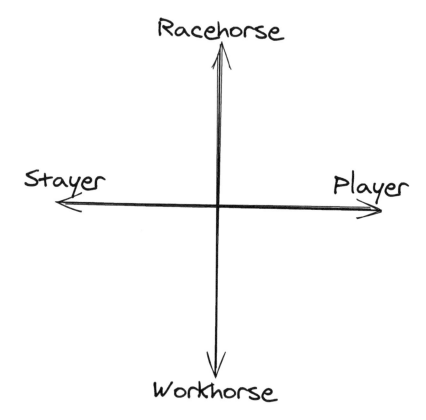

We've overlaid the two dimensions in the diagram above. A candidate who fits on the bottom left might thrive on helping people and providing support to your stakeholders. They are also part of the organisational furniture, love the culture and have no desire to move on. Conversely, you might find a consultant with deep experience in a specific technology at the top right, one who is keenly sought after for high-risk implementations or specific problem-solving. They're a hot commodity thriving on big challenges and short engagements.

PLATFORM ARCHETYPES

Unpacking this model further exposes the nine platform consultant archetypes. Each has distinctive motivators and thus requires different attraction and retention strategies.

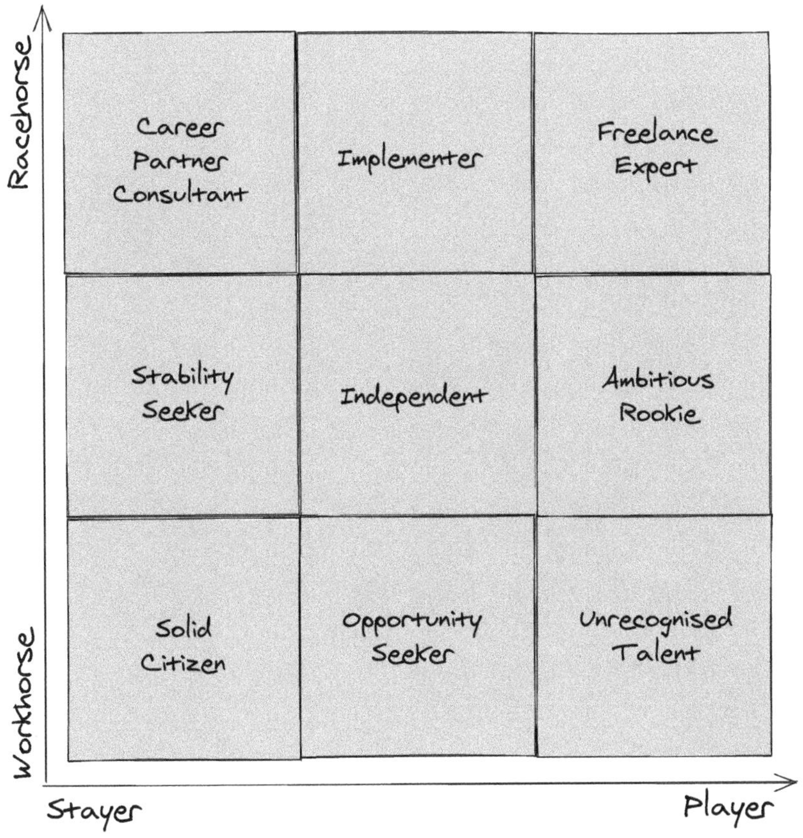

A 3x3 grid. Vertical axis labelled from bottom "Workhorse" to top "Racehorse". Horizontal axis labelled from left "Stayer" to right "Player".

	Stayer		Player
Racehorse	Career Partner Consultant	Implementer	Freelance Expert
	Stability Seeker	Independent	Ambitious Rookie
Workhorse	Solid Citizen	Opportunity Seeker	Unrecognised Talent

The Stayers

Solid Citizens enjoy the operational day-to-day, and they're committed to the organisation for the long haul. They're motivated by solving stakeholder problems and a constant steady stream of learning.

> Stability Seekers like to dive into complex business problems and are happier working on specific pieces of work.

Stability Seekers like to dive into complex business problems and are happier working on specific pieces of work. These individuals may have spent a few years cutting their teeth and climbing the ladder in more high-pressure project-related roles, but now they are after security and longevity with less pressure in their work. Stability Seekers generally prefer project work but are happy to contribute to continuous improvement work – as long as it's skewed towards adding value and building new things more than support. They might have gained experience in big projects or partner world, but they've matured, or their circumstances have changed, meaning they're looking for stability from a permanent role.

Career Partner Consultants love project work and the diversity of clients and problems but prefer the security of a single employer. When partnering with a system integrator, it's these people you rely on to do the heavy lifting on larger pieces of work because they can get in and deliver but won't bounce mid-delivery, leaving you in the lurch. Even though they aren't your direct employees, they still hold IP about your implementation and business, and because they're a stayer, you can feel relatively secure knowing they'll be around your organisation as long as you remain engaged with that partner. That said, not all partner consultants are stayers; many are implementers, so take some time to understand the mix of talent your partner is providing.

The Midfield

Opportunity Seekers are solid team members who are getting itchy feet. While they likely love the company and the work, they're seeking something more. Often they've reached a ceiling in the organisation and feel there is no opportunity for career advancement.

Independents aren't overly motivated by company culture or precious about the type of work. They just here to get the job done. They'll probably be motivated performers and stay as long as you have work for them to do.

Implementers will commit to a project and see it through, but then they're off to the next. They are better suited to large transformation projects because they're unlikely to bounce mid-project but have no desire to hang around after go-live. You'd likely find Implementers as project and program managers.

The Players

Unrecognised Talent refers to those who would make great members of your core team but are ready for a new environment. If you're hiring, then these are great candidates for keeping your stakeholders happy over the long haul. But if they're in your team, there's an issue, and if you don't recognise it and course correct, you may regret losing them.

Ambitious Rookies are happy to jump in to support problems and project

> Unrecognised Talent refers to those who would make great members of your core team but are ready for a new environment.

work. They'd make great core team members, except their ambition to climb the seniority ladder is insatiable. They are a little like the driver who cuts in and out of lanes in traffic.

> If the grad you brought on with high expectations turns out to be a player rather than a stayer, how will you course-correct before losing them to a competitor?

Freelance Experts are the guns for hire. They'll be experts in a niche and bounce between shorter-term engagements. You're unlikely to ever want or need them on your operational team, but in a pinch, they're the people you call on.

ATTRACTION AND RETENTION

At any point in their career, people may move between the different archetypes. For example, an independent expert doesn't start as one. They may begin as an ambitious rookie and end up a stability seeker.

To **attract** the right talent, it is critically important to deeply understand what you need and where your capability is before looking to hire. If you need a solid citizen, you can't afford to pitch the role to an ambitious rookie.

Similarly, to **retain** talent, you'd want to be constantly re-evaluating your team to see if they're moving in a particular direction. If the grad you brought on with high expectations turns out to be a player rather than a stayer, how will you course-correct before losing them to a competitor?

YOUR CORE TEAM

In the last chapter, we introduced the concept of zero-based organisational design – specifically the optimal and project capacity.

To create a cohesive high-performing team, you'll want some stability in the group, so ideally, the bulk of your team will be stayers. That doesn't mean you won't need implementers or experts, but these will be the few rather than the many. The best way to demonstrate this is to overlay the left column in the archetype model with the flex team model.

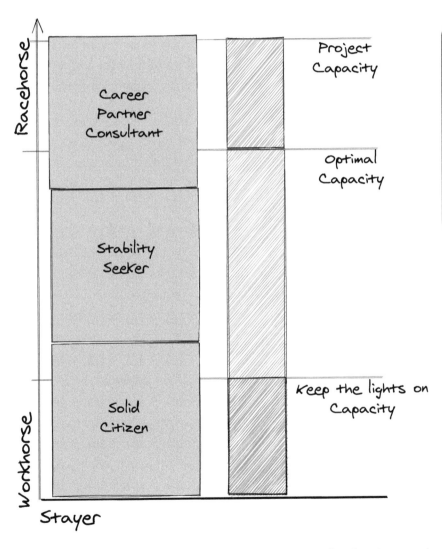

Now that you understand the type of work you need to be done and the archetype that is best suited, you can tailor the candidate search to specific attributes rather than a generic specialist. Similarly, to retain this talent, understanding their individual preferences (remembering these can evolve) puts your team in the best position to ensure your people continue to be involved in work they find motivating.

OPPORTUNITY OR PAUSE FOR CONCERN

Opportunity seekers and unrecognised talent are, in essence, potential great core team members. If they're in the market, they're the type of people you want to attract as they're likely to be loyal and willing to get their hands dirty but have outgrown their current organisation.

If, on the other hand, these people are already in your team, then it's time to course-correct. That doesn't mean creating unnecessary senior roles for the sake of retention (this rarely solves the problem). But it could mean the opportunity to specialise in a particular part of the platform or a lateral move into another role with some new learning. If a conversation with the team member highlights a desire that you cannot accommodate in the organisation, then accept that it's the best thing for them to move on. However, rather than lose them abruptly and interrupt your delivery commitments, consider investing in their learning to prepare them for their move and simultaneously looking for internal talent to step up. If you've nobody ready to step up and your budget allows, go to market early and have them upskill their replacement.

> If a conversation with the team member highlights a desire that you cannot accommodate in the organisation, then accept that it's the best thing for them to move on.

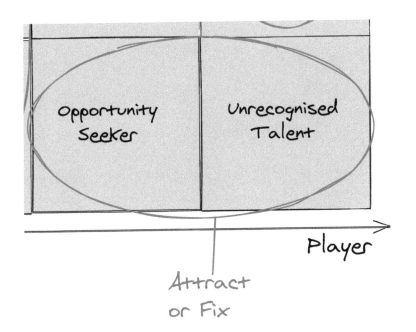

Opportunity Seeker

Unrecognised Talent

Player

Attract or Fix

Independents

Independents are great because they're happy to take on a mix of BAU and project work, and they're willing to hang around – as long as the work is interesting and the day rate keeps up with the market. Of course, you're not committing a permanent role to them, so don't be surprised if and when they chose to move on. Perhaps don't get into a situation where your independents are mission-critical – spread the IP around.

Ambitious rookie

If you've ever managed a grad with two years experience who is struggling

> If you've ever managed a grad with two years experience who is struggling to understand why the CEO hasn't anointed them 2IC, then you're intimately aware of the Ambitious rookie.

> Like the teenager who thinks their parents 'don't get it', the best thing you can do is to let them experience the world.

to understand why the CEO hasn't anointed them 2IC, then you're intimately aware of the Ambitious rookie. They are great to have around the team because they're eager to learn, and, for as long as it is practical, one or two of these energetic people will keep the team on their toes. However, no matter how much learning you think they still have to do (or that you might think you can provide), chances are their expectations of climbing the corporate ladder exceed what you can reasonably support. Like the teenager who thinks their parents 'don't get it', the best thing you can do is to let them experience the world. Their ambition will likely see them jump a few promotions in short succession as they bounce between companies and try their hand at client and vendor side roles. Do what you can to set them up for success, wish them well, and with any luck, you'll be able to get them back one day in the future.

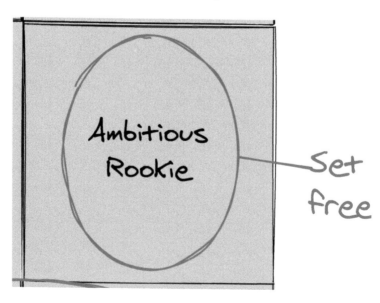

Heavy hitters

Even if you don't own a classic car, you likely know someone who does. At every car show, there are always a couple of hard-core enthusiasts who find each other and begin sharing stories about some esoteric component unique to a certain variant of a particular model from a specific year. Ask them about an issue no mechanic has been able to fix, and it's likely they've dealt with it. Tell them you want to know the go-to person for a factory original restoration, and they'll know the restoration expert. In the platform world, these heavy-hitters are the implementers and the freelance experts, and they aren't typically the roles you advertise for. Most likely, they get their work from referrals, so attracting them is often a case of reaching out to your network or asking your system integrator or vendor for recommendations. Be warned, though; much like tattoos, good work isn't cheap and cheap work isn't good.

It's important to understand the type of work you're looking to kick off with heavy hitters before engaging them. For example, a large transformation project might benefit from an experienced transformation program manager. For this, an implementer is ideal as they're geared towards project engagements, and though they don't want to hang around for the long-term, they will see a program through to implementation.

> Be warned, though; much like tattoos, good work isn't cheap and cheap work isn't good.

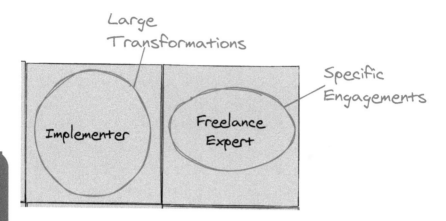

Large Transformations

Implementer

Specific Engagements

Freelance Expert

> To ensure they're around for as long as you need them, you could consider a retention bonus....

The heavy hitters rarely hit your retention radar as they're unlikely to take up a permanent role preferring short-term defined pieces of work. To ensure they're around for as long as you need them, you could consider a retention bonus, but someone who works on a referral basis is unlikely to burn you. In their game, growth lies in their ability to get loyal customers who become, in effect, their marketing department (Reichheld, 2003).

Finding the Opportunity

Simon Balldock, head of Salesforce and Integration at RACV, joined the organisation toward the end of a multi-year, multi-million-dollar transformation project. Charged with taking ownership of the platform just before go-live and building the team to support and enhance the platform, Simon had plenty of work ahead of him.

'To be honest, historically, RACV hasn't had a challenge retaining people. It's the sort of place that people join because they want to be part of an organisation that cares about the community, people

and work-life balance. It's not unusual in this business to come across people with decades of service. But I've found you need to be honest about what you are and what you aren't as an organisation and really specific about the roadmap ahead if you want to find the right fit.

We're never going to be a tech startup wearing t-shirts, shorts and sandals in offices with arcade games and sleeping pods. So I can't compete with people looking for that type of environment. What we have is a community-focused culture, with people who love working for the brand in a large and complex environment. Given the breadth of opportunities in the market, only a small percentage of Salesforce candidates are attracted to a traditional business.

We are also a blended team – a mix of permanent staff and partner consultants, so I need to make sure that everyone's a good fit.

The way I've approached hiring here is to be brutally honest about the type of work we have on our radar and showing a clear vision. There's a lot of hygiene work right now; we're going through an extended stabilisation period. But look how cool this platform is, and you'll get to traverse everything across the entire Salesforce stack so the potential for your experience and your development is massive here. So it's that kind of story.

As for how you retain them? It's about giving them a plan. We're doing an inception phase that gives the team insight into the exciting work ahead and sets an expectation with stakeholders about when we will finish this stabilisation phase and move onto value-added work. But this is all about total transparency of plans and strategy to take it beyond just surviving and on to the next phase.

I think it's also key not to get distracted by the day-to-day and forget about development planning and one-on-ones. I'm talking to the team about finding opportunities to help people grow because there's genuine interest in cross-skilling. It would be too easy to put people in a box and say, 'No. you're just a functional consultant.' But *we have such a complex environment with many many Salesforce products that there's a massive opportunity for people to grow.*

I think the key message is that hiring and retaining good people is all about being honest about the type of work and organisation you are, where your platform is at in its journey, and sometimes turning away the best-qualified candidate because they're not going to be a good fit.'

REFLECTION QUESTIONS:

What does your 24-month roadmap look like?

Does your organisation prefer steady investment and continuous incremental delivery, or is there an appetite for a series of larger, complex, short-term, high-pressure projects?

What type of company culture do you have? Is it a traditional business with long-term employees, shirts and slacks, or a digital company with Silicon Valley-style offices and a constant stream of high-energy aspirational employees?

> The role of any advertising is to attract, not discourage.

Ben Duncombe, the founder of Talent Hub, encourages hiring managers to challenge the traditional recruitment approach and consider 'what is in it for the candidate' rather than 'can you prove this checklist of certification and experience'. The role of any advertising is to attract, not discourage. He poses these questions.

- Why would the suitable and qualified candidates in the market choose your role over others?

- What opportunities will they get at your company that they aren't already getting in their current role?
- What impact can they make in your role and company that they aren't already making?
- How will their skills and knowledge grow and help them achieve their long-term goals?
- Who can they learn from that they don't already have access to?
- How will their career develop with your company differ from where they are?
- What can you offer them that they aren't already being offered? (And not just a pay rise!)
- Are you thinking about all of these aspects when you are trying to find a new team member?

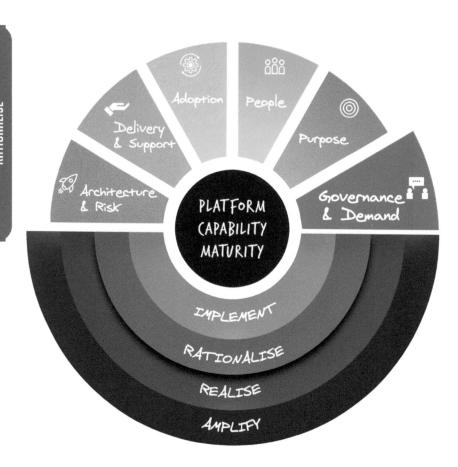

LEVERAGING NETWORKS

THE POWER OF NETWORKING

I once worked for an ultimate networker who had prospered through decades in banking across multiple geographies on the back of 'having chats'. His secret was simple – keep an ear to the ground, be accessible, and always seek to help. He was the champion of hallway networking; even if someone didn't particularly like him, they knew he was a useful guy to know.

> He was the champion of hallway networking; even if someone didn't particularly like him, they knew he was a useful guy to know.

He didn't have to be the smartest person in the room either; for the most part, he didn't have the first clue about the nuts and bolts of how technical things worked, but it didn't matter. His network was his net worth, and he worked it relentlessly.

PLAYING THE GAME

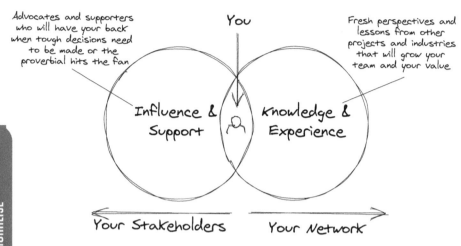

'It's all about the game, and how you play it.'
– The Game, Motörhead 2001.

Like my old boss, your success as a platform owner is largely predicated on the relationships you can leverage.

Let's put you at the centre of a model to explain this. You'll use internal relationships with stakeholders to ensure you're attuned to the pulse of the organisation so you can pivot if necessary but also so you're supported when the shit hits the fan.

Externally your relationships will enable you to keep abreast of the latest trends, learn from others' successes and failures, and bring new thinking and fresh perspectives to the organisation to avoid groupthink and costly mistakes.

INTERNAL STAKEHOLDER RELATIONSHIPS

Plenty has been written about how to manage stakeholders. One of the more common tools is an influence and interest matrix that seeks to quickly establish how much time and effort you might want to give a particular stakeholder.

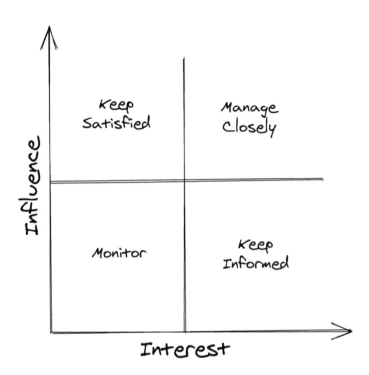

In my experience, this is a good start, but it misses the nuance that some stakeholders are more demanding than others. For example, someone who is highly interested and influential might be a breeze to deal with, trust you implicitly, and be happy to be kept in the loop, whereas you could have someone with very little interest or influence who is simply a nuisance. But ignoring them may backfire.

I think Mitchell, Agle and Wood got closest to describing this phenomenon in their Academy of Management Journal article (Mitchell, 1997). Here's a representation of their model for stakeholder identification and salience.

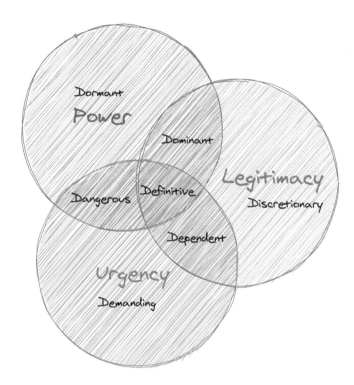

They proposed three attributes of a stakeholder – power, legitimacy and urgency. At the centre of the Venn are the stakeholders who might typically have been at the top right of the previous matrix as those we would manage closely.

However, instead of three other stakeholder groups, they propose six. In complex organisations with politics and hierarchy, I think it's more likely there are seven groups to worry about rather than four.

Dormant stakeholders are worth maintaining a relationship with, mainly because you'd want them in your camp if they were to pick up a second attribute. Let's say a restructure of leadership brought HR under a new leader, and you're accountable for the HRIS platform. Overnight, that previously dormant leader's change in legitimacy makes them a key stakeholder. They might also pick up the attributes of urgency if a budget constraint hit their P&L. The last thing you need is a powerful player becoming dangerous and making noise about the amount of investment in your platform.

Demanding stakeholders are an annoyance because they have no claim to your time, but again, should circumstances change whereby they acquire power, they'll likely seek retribution for being ignored.

Discretionary stakeholders can often get overlooked, which is a ticking time bomb. For example, the IT operations team might legitimately be impacted by the implementation of a new service management platform but lack the power or urgency to warrant the attention of the platform owner who is preoccupied with IT leadership. But when a major incident occurs, and the new tools inhibit their ability to execute effectively on restoring services to customers, they immediately pick up the attribute of urgency and, given the customer impact, also pick up the support of the powerful dormant. They bounce from obscurity to the centre of organisational attention.

How do you solve this? After all, you can't have a personal relationship with everyone. The answer is to be the ultimate networker. Forge strong relationships with the powerful and legitimate and be sure the urgent feel heard. Discuss the claims of the urgent with your powerful and legitimate stakeholders so they know you're listening to those concerns and agree with your approach. If the urgent have a sudden claim to power or legitimacy, your network will support you and your team.

EXTERNAL RELATIONSHIPS

If you consider the value the platform owner brings to the organisation, an adage springs to mind: 'It's who you know, not what.' I'm not about to discount the knowledge and experience you bring to the table, so I prefer to think of it as 'who you know is more important than what you know'.

As far as external relationships are concerned, there are largely four groups:

1. People with the same role (other Platform Owners who may have different titles but have the same remit)

2. People who work in the same industry

3. People who work on the same platform

4. Everyone else you know.

For the purposes of this book, we'll focus on the first three.

As a platform owner, these three groups are an invaluable resource for information and counsel. Let's draw a diagram and break down how you might leverage each of these groups.

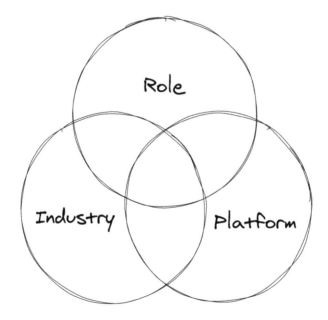

1. People in the same role – Platform approach

How have they tackled similar challenges of platform ownership?

What is their staff retention strategy?

How do they engage partners?

What tips do they have for demand management?

2. *People in your industry – Trends*

What are they seeing and hearing in the market?

What do they see that your organisation has not?

How might you use that intel to bring innovation to your organisation and capitalise on the trend before your competitors do?

3. *People working on the same platform – Inspiration and opportunity*

What projects have they worked on that added value to their organisation?

How did they leverage the platform in a new or innovative way?

What inspiration can you take from these people that creates the next hack-day idea or game-changing innovation in your team?

Who is on the market? What talent can you bring to your team?

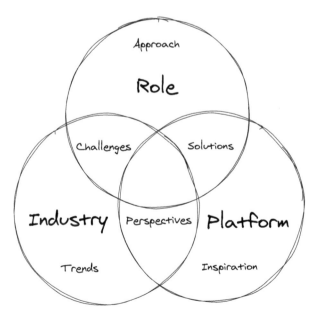

At the intersections of these three groups is where the real magic happens, so let's extend the model.

4. Role and Industry – Challenges

What challenges are they facing that you haven't come across yet?

Do you have any blind spots?

Are you ahead of them, having already solved some of their challenges?

5. Role and platform – Solutions

How have your peers solved the same challenges?

What lessons can you learn from their experience that you'd otherwise learn the hard way?

Where can you save money or time by leveraging their experience?

6. Industry and platform – Perspectives

What do people who operate in your domain (but aren't platform owners) worry about?

How do they see the same challenges through a different lens?

What lessons can you bring back to your team?

What's the benefit of all this external networking? The platform ecosystem is full of people who love to share their successes and ambitions and warn others about the pitfalls. Avoiding costly missed cycles by learning lessons from your peers means you don't distract your team from delivering great work and being recognised for it. Bringing new innovative ideas to the table not

> The platform ecosystem is full of people who love to share their successes and ambitions and warn others about the pitfalls.

only accelerates your personal brand advocacy but prevents your capability from being just a service provider. Instead, it propels you towards Level Three Maturity, where you begin to add more value than your cost base.

Caught up in the day-to-day and distracted by the excitement of working with her exec sponsor and the L&D team on the new initiative, Jennifer has overlooked an important stakeholder.

Paula is well-connected within the organisation. She and the CEO started the same week and have worked in the organisation for more than twenty years. Paula is increasingly unimpressed that her peer, the executive sponsor and Jennifer are running ahead with her idea while ignoring her contribution. Unbeknown to Jennifer, Paula has been sharing growing concerns that this ill-considered rogue project may cause significant change to the business development team and impact new business revenue targets. Even though these are incorrect, the CEO shares Paula's concern, especially as Paula, the head of BD, is his personal friend.

Jennifer is blindsided when the CEO instructs the executive sponsor to shut down the project without further consultation. Jennifer was sure that Paula, who had come up with the idea, was an advocate, but because Paula's team wasn't immediately impacted, she'd neglected to involve her. Instead of recognition and cursory involvement, Paula taught Jennifer a harsh lesson in stakeholder relationship management.

GOVERNANCE & DEMAND

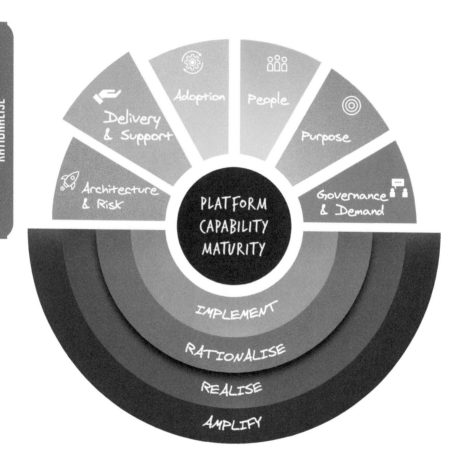

DOGFOODING

Deepika was keen to make an impression and set about looking for ways to improve performance. Her first leadership decision was to structure operational support and feature development into discreet teams. On the surface, this seemed to be a great strategy for ensuring the feature team could demonstrate value through increasing delivery of story points while being shielded from distracting operational support work.

Yet there was a growing number of defects and customer incidents, and the support team was increasingly unable to keep on top of the load – causing some of the team to leave the organisation. Adoption of the platform was beginning to suffer as stability and trust in the data were eroding.

FOUNDATIONS OF PLATFORM SUPPORT

From the day when the first person logs into your platform until the day it is retired, support will be an ongoing requirement. This means a constant juggling of priorities and allocation of capacity to support the solution. As a general rule of thumb, the best practice is to spend no more than 20 per cent of your capacity on support, splitting the remainder between continuous improvement (60 per cent) and innovation (20 per cent). For simplicity, let's call this tension support versus delivery.

> From the day when the first person logs into your platform until the day it is retired, support will be an ongoing requirement.

Generally speaking, platform teams employ two primary models to support their stakeholders. Build-team/run-team or integrated teams.

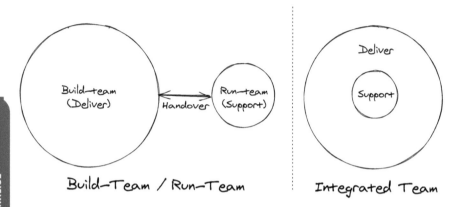

Build-team (Deliver) — Handover → Run-team (Support)

Build–Team / Run–Team

Deliver / Support

Integrated Team

Build-team/run-team essentially means that the platform team is divided into two discreet groups. One group is responsible for new feature development (the build-team) while the other supports and maintains the system (the run-team). During implementation, this might see the partner implementing the solution while the internal team supports the business.

> Integrated team differs in that there may still be two or more groups, but they develop and support their own features or stakeholder groups.

Integrated team differs in that there may still be two or more groups, but they develop and support their own features or stakeholder groups. If an issue arises, then the team who developed the code is accountable to fix it.

We'll demonstrate later that you're not locked into one or another, so if you find one isn't working, you can always pivot to the other. That said, you'll need to pick one and, the collective experience suggests there's a clear winner.

SUPPORT – YOUR PROBLEM OR OUR PROBLEM?

Many organisations subscribe to the build-team/run-team philosophy. On the surface, it seems logical to remove the burden of support from the delivery team and allow them to focus solely on creating value. Some organisations, such as the American market research company Forrester, employ this with relative success.

In a personal interview, Forrester CIO Mike Kasparian argued that the run-team is a good proving ground for new employees and affords them time to learn how the organisation and solution work by supporting it before putting them into the delivery teams. Moreover, this provides the team with career pathways and the ability to take on more graduates.

For Mike and many others, this model works well. However, there are several challenges to consider.

> Many organisations subscribe to the build-team/run-team philosophy. On the surface, it seems logical to remove the burden of support from the delivery team and allow them to focus solely on creating value.

1. When someone knows they're not the one who'll be taking the phone call at 1am or losing a day to resolve an incident caused by poor development practice, they're less likely to ensure their code is thoroughly tested. As a result, quality suffers. This is exacerbated in outsourced and offshore teams.

2. Being removed from the end-user experience breeds a lack of understanding of how the solution is being used by stakeholders, leading to poorer solutions over time.

3. The run team often takes significantly longer to unpick the solution and find the cause of an error because they lack the design context and do not necessarily understand the program logic. Consistent errors and slow turnaround of solutions have a significant impact on adoption.

4. Technology teams are more likely to be engaged if they can be involved in innovative value delivery rather than being stuck solely as the clean-up crew, continually dealing with issues.

> Technology teams are more likely to be engaged if they can be involved in innovative value delivery rather than being stuck solely as the clean-up crew, continually dealing with issues.

As you can see, while providing a training ground for new employees and removing the support burden from your development team seems advantageous on the surface, there are many downsides to consider. In my experience, demonstrated by evidence that you'll see shortly, there is a better way.

EAT YOUR OWN DOG FOOD

Have you ever heard of the terms 'food taster' or 'cup bearer'? Roman Emperors, Egyptian Pharaohs, various royalty and even dictators used human guinea pigs, often slaves, known as 'praegustators', to consume a small portion of their meal or beverage to ensure it was free of poison. As recently as 2014, Vladimir Putin was reported to employ a full-time food taster (Walsh, 2014). The medieval Jewish philosopher Maimonides (1134-1204) described Kings forcing their cooks to eat a portion of the meal they had prepared.

This concept of the chef being required to eat the meal they prepared to prove its utility is a great analogy for good platform development practices. Fundamentally, high performing platform teams operate on the premise of ownership. The key to achieving that ownership is to employ the integrated team model.

This requires the team, during sprint planning, to commit to delivering an amount of backlog work that will take 60-80 per cent of their capacity, leaving the remainder for innovation and support. At each sprint, one team member is allocated the role of monitoring support requests, and they judge who is best placed to pick up the support and distribute it. In the ideal scenario where less than 20 per cent of capacity is required for support, you, as the diligent platform owner, have ensured that there's additional scoped work ready for the team to pick up should they complete their committed work.

For clarity, this doesn't mean you can't or shouldn't have admins who pick up and execute admin work. It would be counterintuitive and costly to distract your development team with admin work. The point, though, is that your team should be owning and maintaining their code.

> It would be counterintuitive and costly to distract your development team with admin work. The point, though, is that your team should be owning and maintaining their code.

PROOF IN THE PUDDING

For your developers, being closer to the stakeholders and how they use the platform, coupled with the responsibility for resolving any coding issues with which they're already familiar, results in

> For your developers, being closer to the stakeholders and how they use the platform, coupled with the responsibility for resolving any coding issues with which they're already familiar, results in higher quality solutions and faster turnaround for remediation.

higher quality solutions and faster turnaround for remediation. And that, in turn, creates higher stakeholder engagement and increased value. In early 2016, PagerDuty, a US-based SaaS incident response platform provider, pivoted to this model with remarkable results. Integrating development and operations improved time to market, innovation and quality. Specifically, they achieved a 45 per cent increase in the number of changes deployed to production, 25 per cent reduction in significant incidents that impact customers and a 50 per cent reduction in Mean Time To Resolution (MTTR) of major incidents (Armandpour, 2017).

Significantly more features were delivered with fewer errors, and the time to resolve issues halved. That sounds like the way to go, don't you think?

Fiona, one of the few remaining senior support people in Deepika's team, had enough, found another role, and resigned. No longer burdened with the fear of repercussions for upsetting management, she called a town hall with Deepika and the leadership team and laid out the facts. The entire team was looking for other opportunities, incident rates were increasing, and customer satisfaction was dropping. Moreover, the dev's weren't shielded from the support work because the run team was constantly interrupting them for assistance to debug the solution. Asked what she'd do differently, Fiona proposed an immediate plan to integrate the teams. She spent the remainder of her notice period overhauling the ways of working. As a result, team happiness skyrocketed, and there were immediate reductions in defects and outages. During Fiona's farewell speech, Deepika apologised for letting the team down and thanked Fiona for her work reinvigorating the team. Deepika openly shared her embarrassment and sadness as she lamented losing Fiona from the team and committed to keeping the door remained open should Fiona ever want to return.

Fiona was back the following Monday and was still with the organisation several years later.

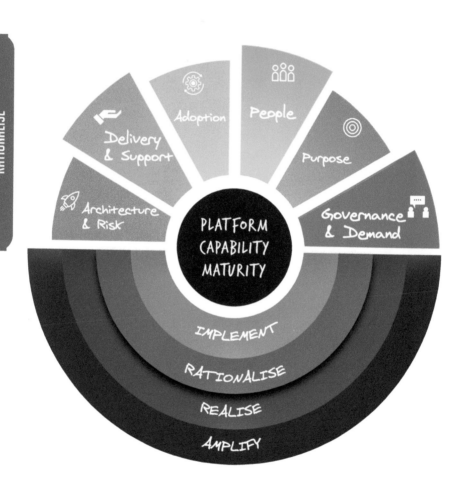

Delivery & Support

Adoption

People

Purpose

Architecture & Risk

PLATFORM CAPABILITY MATURITY

Governance & Demand

IMPLEMENT

RATIONALISE

REALISE

AMPLIFY

FINDING THE RIGHT ANSWER

IN SEARCH OF A SOLUTION

When you're designing solutions, it turns out everyone looks at a problem slightly differently, with a different set of experiences and perspectives. If your newly formed team, with minimal context, was asked to solve the same problem with all the same information, each person would almost certainly offer a unique solution. Conversely, a group who had been working together for quite a while and all had the same context might land on very similar solutions or, worse, defer the decision to a single anointed individual. With multiple options to choose from or a single unquestionable option, how do you know you've got the best answer to the problem?

SURELY ANY ANSWER WILL DO?

Being presented with multiple solutions provides an interesting challenge. Looking to pick the 'right answer' is a trap as it implies that all or any answers are incorrect. However, assuming the individuals have appropriate skills, experience and training, it's likely that most of the solutions proposed would have proved perfectly functional, and no single solution will be perfect. And since no one solution will be perfect, a single unchallenged option will inevitably be functional but sub-optimal, perhaps even risky. Therefore, platform teams ought to search for the optimal solution, which is fit for purpose (note I didn't say perfect). But finding

> Being presented with multiple solutions provides an interesting challenge. Looking to pick the 'right answer' is a trap as it implies that all or any answers are incorrect.

the optimal solution is a conundrum of human rather than technical complexity.

FINDING OPTIMAL

The first university subject I ever attended was 'information systems risk and security'. The content was as dry as you could imagine, a matter of remembering a raft of Australian and international risk management standards and knowing where to apply them. Endre Bihari, the lecturer, was one of the most memorable characters of my uni days. He suffered no fools, but he was, I felt, genuinely keen to see those who put in the work succeed. He was great at telling stories that, if you paid attention, led to a deep-thinking crescendo. What we learned in that class was far more valuable than what the curriculum was set to teach. Critical thinking has served all my teams well over the following decade. Endre's mantra was repeated ad nauseum, 'check your assumptions'.

> Deciding on the optimal solution is where the magic lies, as it's often a combination of elements from all the proposed solutions.

Deciding on the optimal solution is where the magic lies, as it's often a combination of elements from all the proposed solutions. It will consider multiple technical approaches as well as speed to deliver, scalability, usability and risk. To approach this needs a little dose of what Jerry Hirshberg, author and founder of Nissan Design International, describes as creative abrasion (Hirshberg, 1998).

I'd spend the week between Endre's lectures pondering something, unpicking it from as many angles as I could. I would debate colleagues at work or fellow students in the library until I was absolutely certain I had the answer. My measure was to be sure I could not be convinced otherwise. Inevitably, Endre would pick the argument apart with as few as two and no more than five pointed questions. On one occasion, he could have nailed it with a single question, but he always started with 'Have you checked your assumptions?' It took the entire 12 weeks of that university semester, but I learned a valuable lesson. My role as a leader wasn't to be right – it was to make sure every angle was considered, and every assumption checked.

In the context of your platform team, this can be a regular team ritual where each request or feature is discussed as a group. The owner of the work describes how they intend to solve the problem, and the solution is peer-reviewed to reach an optimal solution. This process would consider technical, usability and delivery perspectives. Often the debate will not conclude in one sitting – the team may decide it makes sense to test a few assumptions or options programmatically and report back to conclude the debate.

EASIER SAID THAN DONE

Clive came on the scene around the same time as Endre. He was appointed Director of Shared Services – a nice title designed to mask that a huge restructure was upon us. Through an unlikely sequence of events, I landed on the better side of the restructure equation, and Clive went so far as to give me a go in one of his leadership positions. He even appointed a personal mentor for my first year. On the one hand, he'd taken a punt on me, yet on the other, I really had to earn it. While my mentor voluntarily moved on after six months because he felt I had things in hand, Clive relentlessly questioned every decision; his favourite line was, 'That doesn't make sense to me'. I constantly felt inadequate, and my self-doubt increased day by day. I'd work late nights (on top of the uni work) and most weekends, preparing Excel worksheets and PowerPoint documents. Had I not been so stubborn, I'd have resigned. After all, I'd worked there ten years by this stage and had seen many of the pricks come, give me a hard time, and go. This guy wouldn't break me.

> Not everybody is comfortable with being challenged – at least not initially.

Not everybody is comfortable with being challenged – at least not initially. Often platform teams are formed from people with diverse cultural backgrounds, and while some cultures and personality types thrive on open debate, others struggle. Moreover, in some cultures, critical questions might be considered disrespectful. While we want to encourage critical thinking, the last thing we want is a manager or strong personality asking a question that causes someone to shut down rather than give the positive response necessary for solving complex problems.

Achieving the best outcomes through open debate requires the participants to feel psychologically safe. In her book, *The Fearless Organization,* Amy C Edmondson describes psychological safety as the shared feeling that you can express your thoughts and ideas, make mistakes, and ask for help without receiving negative reactions. This requires the group leader to reframe their role from authority to directing the team toward goals and encouraging ideas, focusing on learning and rewarding those who speak up about risks and opportunities (Edmondson, 2018).

One day on the weekly red-eye flight to Sydney, somewhere between 'Does anybody need a headset' and 'Please return your seat to its upright position', I had an odd realisation. Clive had stopped being interested in every minute detail of my decisions. The past few meetings could even have been described as painless. Over dinner, I had to find out, had he just given up and was ready to punt me out the door, or was he distracted elsewhere? To his credit, he is the sort of chap you can be blunt with, so I straight out asked if my time was up. His face was priceless, a stunned look somewhere between amused and disappointed. Clive shared a story about how he and his Dad loved to debate topics – often deliberately taking a position opposite to their personal viewpoint, just for the sake of debating. At the end of the story, he concluded by saying that his nature was to question until the questions ran out. Since he felt I now 'got it', he didn't need to question anymore. My apprenticeship was complete. From that point on, we debated everything, but my energy was different.

When Clive was pushing me that year, he had nothing but good intentions. But for a long time, I was left with a strong feeling of being wrong or not good enough no matter what I did. This despite the fact that he was simply expanding my thinking. The lesson here is the importance of trust and being deliberate and open about your process and intentions – to challenge the thinking, not the person and to be sure they know this is the case.

> The lesson here is the importance of trust and being deliberate and open about your process and intentions – to challenge the thinking, not the person and to be sure they know this is the case.

'There's no team without trust.'
– Paul Santagata, Head of Industry at Google.

THE MANTRA

I refer to meetings where platform teams discuss and debate as 'design sessions'. I have a mantra repeated at the opening of each session as a ritual; 'We challenge the solution, not the person.' It feels a little odd at first, but setting the scene reminds everyone that their role is to solicit perspectives from their peers, call out any unproductive behaviour and land on the optimal solution. That doesn't mean there shouldn't be a rigorous debate but that everyone should feel fearless. The model below demonstrates this.

DEALING WITH THE STALEMATE

Occasionally, but hopefully, not too often, you might end up with two reasonable alternative options, each with its own costs and consequences. If different individuals champion those solutions, this puts you back into a win-lose situation. In this case, a decision framework may prove beneficial. That involves making a call about who the decision-maker is and having the team confirm that, while they won't necessarily agree with a decision, they will accept and support the decision and the consequences. Ideally, this is a team member involved rather than management, and importantly it shouldn't always be the same person. Once a decision is made – even if the results turn bad – 'I told you so' must never enter the conversation. After all, the alternative may have also failed. Instead, the team sees this as a learning opportunity and rallies to collectively resolve or back out of the problem.

> Once a decision is made – even if the results turn bad – 'I told you so' must never enter the conversation. After all, the alternative may have also failed.

David Dawson, Engineering Lead at ANZ Bank, described the decision framework as a game-changer. 'I'm not a naturally confrontational person, but I know when there's a good technical reason for a decision, and I will fight for it. I once worked at a large tech organisation where the culture actively encouraged robust conversations that challenged and validated solutions. That meant people from all over the company with strong engineering knowledge but without deep platform-specific experience could offer opinions on technical decisions.

Primarily this worked well because it kept us continually checking our biases. But there was a period where I worked with some strong characters who held contrary opinions on architecture which was my accountability. When working with these strong personalities, it took a great deal of energy to get a decision across the line. The conversations were always professional, but I think the team felt there were a few personal crusades at play. These debates became so exhausting that I seriously considered leaving the company.

Over drinks, one Friday, a new team member commented that the conversations seemed equally valuable when our executive manager was there, but much shorter and less exhausting. It seems obvious now, but it took a fresh set of eyes to point out that when he was there, things were different. We were improving each other's ideas while making individual cases because we deferred the decision to him and supported the outcome regardless. As peers, when he wasn't around, we spent more time advocating alternate perspectives and battling for a win-lose.

Just as we had the epiphany, the organisation instigated a company-wide decision framework, essentially requiring us to be explicit about who would be consulted and who would decide on a solution. There was an immediate behaviour change when everyone was clear on who the decider was. Decisions were made far faster without relying on one default decision-maker for everything. At that point, the boss was a rarely needed escalation point for when we couldn't agree who would decide.'

REAPING THE REWARDS

There have been many studies on the impacts of critical thinking and psychological safety on team performance. Perhaps most famous is 'Project Aristotle', the multi-year study of team effectiveness across 180 teams at Google. It analysed numerous factors that might explain why some teams performed better than others, including education, background, personality traits, incentivisation, shared interests, and whether they socialised together. The study found no correlating features, but psychological safety was concluded as the key factor that led to high performance in teams (Duhigg, 2016).

REFLECTION QUESTIONS:

Have the team(s) developed a safe environment where they are comfortable to have robust conversations without fear?

Does the team have rituals where team members are encouraged to discuss their approach to solving specific business problems and allowing peers to challenge the solution?

Have the team(s) agreed with a decision-making framework to enable them to move forward without the need for escalation?

PEOPLE | DELIVER & SUPPORT | GOVERNANCE & DEMAND

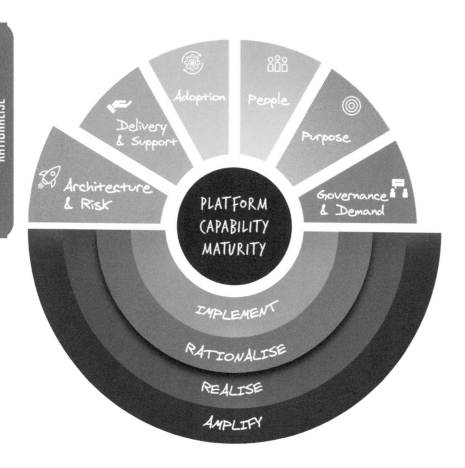

BALANCING DEBT

The head of customer acquisition at Jennifer's company was already having a bad week, and today's quarterly governance meeting wasn't going well. 'We were promised increased speed to market once we'd replaced the legacy system, yet so far, all I hear are excuses for why each request is so hard. I was beginning to think this platform is a piece of s**t, but my partner's firm runs the same platform, and they're kicking goals, so clearly you guys don't know what you're doing.'

It was an unfair assessment, but on the surface, not a difficult conclusion to draw. After all, the platform had been in for six months now, but seemingly routine requests were increasingly difficult to deliver.

SOME DEBT IS GOOD, BUT BE SURE TO MAKE YOUR REPAYMENTS

 PRO-TIP

I'm going to incite the agile purists here, but hear me out.

If you're reading this from a software engineering background, then the title alone has probably started your blood boiling. Please understand that I'm abundantly aware of Ward Cunningham's use of the loan metaphor to describe refactoring as not just polishing code but instead completing the code by better understanding the problem or domain. Doug Knesek has a great series on that on LinkedIn (Knesek, 2016). I'm deliberately choosing to use the contemporary interpretation, though I'm not advocating for anarchy.

Why am I doing this? Because, in reality, many people

reading this book will enter a Maturity Level Two situation by inheriting a platform beyond the initial implementation or simply because the platform implementations rarely live in a theoretical purist agile software engineering world with zero debt. I need an analogy most people will understand.

If you've come to platform ownership from a different angle and have never heard of Ward Cunningham or extreme programming, then all you really need to know is that I'm re-using an analogy from one of the first Agile projects in a way that is completely at odds with the intent of the chap who first used it; just because I can.

Remember we mentioned the butterfly effect at Maturity Level One? Making a tactical decision has consequences for the future. During the implementation phase, corners are cut, and requirements de-scoped. Typically it happens for seemingly valid reasons, but now you're here at Level Two, these truths begin to surface.

> Making a tactical decision has consequences for the future. During the implementation phase, corners are cut, and requirements de-scoped.

The agile software engineering community refers to these issues as 'technical debt' and, like any debt, it needs to be repaid – generally with interest.

That said, I don't subscribe to the assertion of some developers that tech debt is all bad and must be eliminated. I believe, like any debt, you have a choice. You can choose to repay some and accrue new ones. Like financial debt, it's about making smart investments and understanding debt dynamics.

DEBT DYNAMICS

Most people are familiar with the concept of a credit card. You don't have the cash to pay for something, but you can still have the goods or service immediately so long as you commit to your credit provider to pay it back quickly after that and/or to pay some interest.

Software development isn't as simple as picking up a new pair of heels at the store and popping it on the card, but some dynamics are similar. Let's say we have a competitor release a new product to market, and our executive team needs everyone to scramble so we don't lose any market share. There are two ways we can get the same capability to market, one follows all our sound design principles and scales infinitely but will take six months to get to market; the other gets a product to market in six weeks, it will still be secure and functional but won't scale beyond a single product. The risk of the latter is that there's a good chance that soon after we release our new product, the competitor will pivot, and we won't be able to. There's also an overhead cost to running the tactical solution while developing the strategic one. However, the opportunity cost of waiting is high; our customers are likely to jump ship if we don't have this capability fairly rapidly, and the acquisition cost is 10x retention. What do we do?

It's a real and constant battle to accommodate business imperatives while ensuring the continued ability to scale and pivot. Some die-hard agilists would argue that tech debt cannot be accepted under any circumstances. But as Dan Radigan at Atlassian states, 'Technical debt is a reality for all software teams. Nobody avoids it entirely – the main thing is to keep it from spiralling out of control' (Radigan, n.d.).

GETTING READY FOR SCALE

You might recall the scaffold analogy in the introduction to the book. One of the roles of scaffolding is to provide stability to the building, but it doesn't come from the scaffolding alone. Another important feature of building is ensuring that you have a solid foundation. As you leave the implementation phase (or land in the platform owner role, post-implementation), it's good to take stock of the situation and shore up the foundations. It will be critical to enable the platform to scale. You don't want to add an additional storey to the building, then discover the footings were built incorrectly, make the building unsafe, and requiring considerable repair time. Worse still, what if there was a total building collapse?

Take the opportunity to audit the environment(s), perhaps consider using a partner or see if your vendor provides health check services as part of your subscription. Review the project working group and steering committee updates looking for issues and descoped items, and check these are still valid with your stakeholders. If the project team members are still around, ask them where the skeletons are buried. You're looking to build a list of remediation items into your backlog.

> If you can get away with it, you might want to consider a few sprints of remediation work before taking on any new feature or project activity.

If you can get away with it, you might want to consider a few sprints of remediation work before taking on any new feature or project activity. The more solid your foundation, the faster you'll be able to scale the solution. I once thought that asking the team to pick up tech debt cards in a sprint would be met with disdain. However, generally speaking, team members are tired of running up against tech debt challenges when trying to deliver value and relish the opportunity to spend some time solving the problems that give them constant headaches.

Beyond an initial cleanup, you'll want to be sure you commit to cleaning up a number of these items in each future iteration or sprint. Like your bank loan, the interest compounds, so keep making repayments. A good rule of thumb is that at least five to ten per cent of your sprint commitment should be to clean up tech debt. Let the team pick the ones they most want to tackle.

> A good rule of thumb is that at least five to ten per cent of your sprint commitment should be to clean up tech debt.

At Australian real estate advertising portal realestate.com.au the platform team hived off ten per cent of their engineering effort over several months to convert their Salesforce environment to DX – a set of tools from Salesforce designed to enable agile processes for developers on their platform (Crozier, 2018). Using this technology, the platform team established a continuous integration environment that accelerated their deployments by 330 per cent, not bad considering their target was 60 per cent. This improvement also allowed them to invest more time to remediate technical debt and free up more time for experimentation without impacting delivery commitments.

TAKING ON DEBT

For the first twenty years of the 21st century in Australia, just about anyone could take out a loan and buy property. A government inquiry into the banking sector shut down a lot of that bad lending behaviour, and there are now more rigorous checks and balances. These days, generally speaking, only if you can prove you have the means to live and make repayments will you be offered credit. If we liken the debt audit and cleanup to the government review, then it is now your job to ensure debt lending in your platform environment remains in check.

PRO-TIP

Some questions to ask:

Is this tactical shortcut worth the cost? What is the impact of running with the debt added to the cost to pay it down, measured against the reward?

Have we considered the impact of this on top of existing debt? Do we have the requisite skills and capacity to pay it down?

Does a win in one area of my business create a cost in another? Is the entire business aware of (and accepting) the impact?

In summary, make a **conscious** decision if you wish to take a shortcut or defer something. You will need to commit to fixing it later or feel the pain of compounding interest. It doesn't take long for interest to become crippling.

Jennifer got the team together for a day of planning. They began with a retrospective and highlighted three key themes.

1. *Growing noise in the business about speed to deliver*
2. *Continued expectation of cutting corners to meet deadlines*
3. *Workarounds on top of workarounds making delivery of new features increasingly challenging.*

Jennifer and the leadership worked through four key objectives.

The first involved dedicating capacity and asking their implementation partner to dive into the system and review the depth of the problems.

The second meant negotiating a one month hold on new features to allow the team to make a significant dent in remediating the issue.

The third required implementing a more rigorous process for accruing new debt that would include the voice of the engineering team before commitments were made to the business.

The outcome was to implement measures and dedicate capacity for ongoing tech debt remediation.

Jennifer had a big task ahead to negotiate with the executive to get buy-in to these plans. The head of customer acquisition was sceptical about the capability of the platform team and reluctant to agree to pause development. However, the CEO decided that doing nothing and expecting a different outcome was insane, so he granted Jennifer's requests.

Morale in the team immediately skyrocketed. Not only could they focus an entire month on complex challenges that plagued them daily, but they gamified it, challenging each other to squash more bugs. Together they redesigned and refactored entire components of the platform. Moreover, their voices were heard before work was committed, and they could continually refactor work.

Jennifer was able to show management the metrics for feature throughput before and after the cleanup exercise. This kicked off the discussion about the cost of taking shortcuts and opened the door to more robust conversations about considering the cost versus reward of future decisions. Throughput increased by 43 per cent and was maintained for three years.

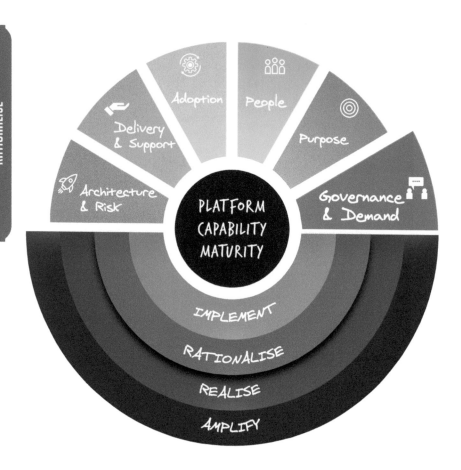

KEEP IT SIMPLE(R)

'Seriously, Deepika, this process is bullshit...' began one of Deepika's lead consultants. 'It's so broken that the onboarding experience is embarrassing.' Deepika had been progressively onboarding new team members but was not close to the detail. Deepika's lead BA chimed in, 'Tell me about it, I've been here six months, and yesterday I got an email from HR telling me that they would escalate to my manager if I didn't complete compliance training. But it was the first time I'd ever heard about it.'

Deepika canvassed a few more of her team and realised the challenge was an ongoing source of frustration in the organisation, particularly across the retail stores, but it was largely unaddressed because no single department owned the problem.

MORE VALUE, LESS EFFORT

Sometimes the greatest value a platform owner can add to the organisation goes beyond the platform's boundaries. It takes a keen eye to look around at what's not working for the organisation to realise the benefits of the platform capability.

> Sometimes the greatest value a platform owner can add to the organisation goes beyond the platform's boundaries.

Do you recall remote working during the COVID-19 pandemic? Many organisations were forced to close offices, and without much preparation, people began working from home. What was initially expected to be a couple of weeks became, in some cases, many long months of isolation.

While some businesses found that employee productivity increased, many reported marked decreases in productivity. I spoke to a manager concerned that a colleague who was usually his highest performer had 'slacked off' during the pandemic. I encouraged him to challenge his assumptions and dig under the surface. It turned out that this chap was a master at his role because he knew how to manually bypass organisational roadblocks and spent many hours each day walking between buildings and offices to get the paperwork through rigorous disjointed approval processes. Without the ability to desk stop people and manually extract signatures, he was forced to go through digital channels and became frustratingly inefficient.

With this observation, you could dive straight into migrating the process into an electronic approval system but, as a platform owner, there's often a way to bring more value with less development effort.

WHY NOT JUST CODE IT?

Any inefficient process remains inefficient unless it's redesigned. At a glance, a good analyst would recognise that a process that was organically developed and fundamentally designed on the premise that people would be in a physical location is bound to perform poorly – even if it is systemised. Therefore, we need to provide more value than just writing software to deliver the maximum return.

BECOMING AN INTERNAL CONSULTANCY

It's time to become more than just a software development house. Evolving to an internal consultancy allows you to bring significantly more value to the table. One of the easiest ways your capability can provide consultancy to your stakeholders is through providing business process optimisation capability. This means dedicating time to seek out and streamline broken or inefficient business processes, with development delivering only the last mile. Imagine making a business process 50 per cent more efficient and improving customer sentiment by 20 percentage points when all you had to do was make a couple of quick changes in the platform to accommodate a reordered workflow? It seems like a smarter investment than coding a fully electronic workflow system that remained as inefficient as the previous process and delivered little value.

Process and quality improvement methodologies took off in Japan in the 1970s and provided them with a game-changing competitive advantage. These underpinned their ability to produce low-cost quality products and dominate key industries such as consumer electronics, telecommunications and vehicles.

Lean, Six Sigma and Kaizen are all examples of techniques and tools used for this purpose. Check out iassc.org for more details on these.

Flawed processes generally build organically over time. By way of example, have you ever tried producing reporting for an executive? They start with a vague idea of what they're after, you beaver away making numbers, and over a series of cycles, the report becomes a behemoth as each iteration raises more questions and requires more analysis and data. At some point in the process, the original intention is either answered or lost. But once you've opened Pandora's Box, every look at the numbers produces more intrigue and a desire for a different cut or deeper analysis on a metric. It's a rabbit hole. I've found that processes in larger and mature organisations tend to suffer the same fate. They get built organically over years (or decades), and each time one minor

> Flawed processes generally build organically over time. By way of example, have you ever tried producing reporting for an executive?

incident happens or a new regulation comes in, an additional task or check comes into the process. Over time these small changes add a significant overhead to these processes.

You'll find that you can add a significant amount of value with two relatively simple steps

...each time one minor incident happens or a new regulation comes in, an additional task or check comes into the process. Over time these small changes add a significant overhead to these processes.

1. Reorder the actions to remove handovers because each time something moves between people, you add elapsed time to the process. If one person or group is involved multiple times in a process, then combine the tasks. Even better, can one team pick up more tasks in the sequence rather than hand them over at all?

2. Question the relevance of an action. If nobody remembers why we do it, it's probably ripe for cutting.

I once heard the story of a farewell at a large Australian bank. This chap had worked in the organisation for more than forty years, so when he retired, the leadership called an all-hands meeting, got cake and made speeches. A tradition at the bank was for the retiring employee to run through a short history of their career highlights – somewhat akin to a eulogy (presumably to inspire the younger recruits to aspire to a lifetime in the institution).

The retiree began by recalling how he'd joined the bank as a teller in a rough part of town in the 1960s and had been held up at least once by armed bandits. He ended by describing his last nine years as his

MATURITY LEVEL TWO
RATIONALISE

proudest, where he was entrusted to produce a detailed daily report exclusively for the CEO. It took the entire day to produce and was critical to the CEO's ability to manage the media and the board. The report was so sensitive that it had to be printed and hand-delivered.

The CEO had been messing about on his phone at the back of the room when mention of his name grabbed his attention. He'd been in the role for five years and thought he'd better make specific mention of the report in his thank-you speech. He asked his assistant which report the veteran was referring to. His EA replied, 'I doubt you've ever seen it, your predecessor never read it, so I just put it in the shredder each morning.'

DOES BUSINESS PROCESS OPTIMISATION REALLY ADD THAT MUCH VALUE?

A 2011 case study of applying lean principles to new product development led to a reduction of cycle time by 32 per cent (Rajesh Solanki, 2011). Moreover, a 2017 study found that applying six sigma to sales and marketing processes improved decision-making and sustained revenue growth during market uncertainty (Madhani, 2017).

In 2018 I had the opportunity to work with two inspiring women, Dominique Franco and Rachel Brennan-Behan of REA Group, who, fuelled by personal frustration and falling customer sentiment, initiated a review of the end-to-end customer contracting and onboarding process. Applying the lean principles bestowed on them by productivity blogger and Chief Inventor Nigel Dalton, the team refactored the business process with dramatic results. Requiring almost no technology change, the team removed an entire legacy system from the process, removed 80 per cent of data rekeying, centralised the processing work into a single team removing several handovers, and reduced the processing time from four days down to one, thereby doubling customer satisfaction.

DON'T LET THESE WINS GO UNNOTICED

Unlike big project launches or major enhancements to your platform, these process improvements can go largely unnoticed, yet cumulatively these can add significant business value over a year. So it's on you to make sure you're communicating widely and loudly about them. Testimonials are always good for this, where someone explains with real metrics how much better their life is or the significant improvement it has made to customer experience. Communicating these wins is all about building efficacy for your platform teams brand and taking you closer to Level Three – Realise.

> Communicating these wins is all about building efficacy for your platform teams brand and taking you closer to Level Three – Realise.

Onboarding was indeed a complex set of handoffs between departments with manual, largely undocumented, processes. The business had grown rapidly over the past twelve months, and the processes were not coping.

Deepika was keen to build a relationship with the Chief People Officer and offered to take ownership of creating a transparent, scalable solution if the CPO was willing to be the project sponsor. Best of all, Deepika was convinced it would take little development work and could be squeezed into her continuous improvement backlog.

Over four workshops, Deepkia's BA unpacked the process and proceeded to remove many of the handovers and waste. The developers built a simple integration from the HRIS to the ITSM tooling that allowed the process to trigger off tasks to the key players, and a couple of basic workflows facilitated most tasks that needed no human intervention.

The CPO was ecstatic with the results. Feedback from the retail leaders was phenomenal, and HR shuffled some of their team's admin roles to dedicate an additional person in the Talent Acquisition team to cope with the increasing demand. The technology support team was now aware up to eight weeks ahead of new employees starting and proactively had the equipment and system access ready before their arrival. The team responsible for ensuring all new employees had completed onboarding compliance training saw an improvement in completing onboarding tasks to 90 per cent within seven days. It was a massive change from 20 per cent in thirty days.

With four hours of workshops and three days of development, Deepika's team added significant material value to the organisation, and her CPO was more than happy to tell all her executive-level peers about it.

GOVERNANCE & DEMAND

PART TWO
STRATEGIC VALUE

	Maturity	$ROI	Effort : Return
Strategic Value ↑	Amplify	× 10	1 : 20
	Realise	× 5	1 : 10
	— — — Tipping Point — — —		
Operational Value ↑	Rationalise	× 1	1 : 1
	Implement	× 0.5	2 : 1

MATURITY LEVEL THREE
REALISE

You've recently emerged from Level Two, and your house is now in order. You have a good team that is clear on what needs doing and how to do it. You have a strong stakeholder group that trusts and supports you, and your platform technical debt is manageable. Time to kick back and relax, right?

Nope. You've reached the tipping point. Welcome to the starting line.

Up to this point, your platform and capability were delivering, at best, operational value. You've just completed pre-season training and are ready to roll up to day one in the majors. No time for slacking; you need to double down. It's time to deliver strategic value.

So, where do we start? How about proving you're worthy of your place as team captain. It's time to show them what you bring to the table.

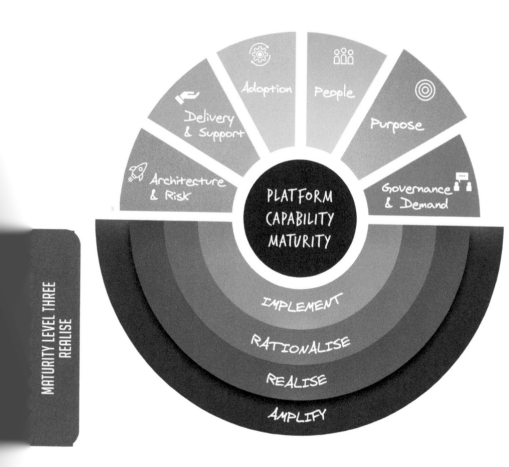

MATURITY LEVEL THREE
REALISE

PLATFORM
CAPABILITY
MATURITY

Adoption

People

Delivery
& Support

Purpose

Architecture
& Risk

Governance
& Demand

IMPLEMENT

RATIONALISE

REALISE

AMPLIFY

SHOW ME THE ~~MONEY~~ VALUE

> *Lucas's team delivered the first major enhancement to the platform since the project; a shiny new module in the HRIS allowing managers to track career goals and development plans. The head of L&D championed the initiative and was convinced that it would show the power of the new platform and start demonstrating the value of the investment.*
>
> *A few managers got on board, but most did the bare minimum to meet their KPI reporting to ensure everyone had a plan in the system. The tech did what it said on the box, but while it was exactly what the sponsor ordered, it was hardly a game-changer.*

VALUE BEYOND DELIVERY

You might have heard the infamous innovation quote attributed to Henry Ford, 'If I had asked people what they wanted, they would have said faster horses.' Why is this relevant? Because often, your stakeholders won't always know what they need. It's your role to help them find the answer.

STEPPING UP

There are a couple of reasons why you'll want to take a leadership position at Level Three.

The first is internally focused. Your stakeholders don't know what they don't know. When it comes to the capabilities of your platform, they're unconsciously incompetent. If they ask you to 'Build x', then, by and large, the solution will only leverage the capabilities they understand. On the other hand, you are sitting on a wealth of knowledge between yourself, your team, and your network.

PURPOSE

Second, if you focus externally, genuine competitors will likely have access to the same platforms as you. Your competitive advantage doesn't come from having the platform alone; it's how you are more innovative with it.

In essence, you're sitting on a rocket with endless capabilities, but if you don't take control of the launch codes, then either nobody will get the benefit of launching a missile or someone unqualified will do so and cause a disaster.

So how do you change the game? Stop being subservient.

TAKING THE REINS

The process of realising value from your platform is evolutionary. Let's draw this up as a model.

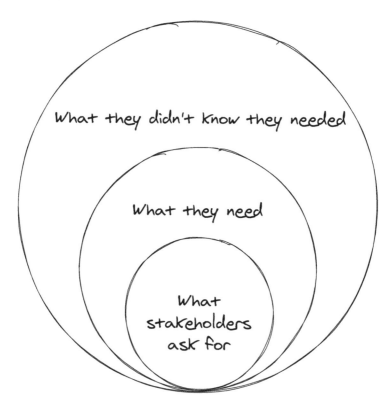

At Level One, you delivered what was asked for. Stakeholders dictated what they wanted, and you made it a reality. By Maturity Level Two, you changed the conversation from 'What do you want?' to 'What do you need?' – or even better, 'What problem are you trying to solve and what outcome are you seeking'. You found this approach led to significantly improved solutions successfully solving customer problems because your team understands your platform capabilities better than anyone in the organisation. So when you focus on solving problems rather than turning out widgets, you achieve better results and have happier staff. You give them what they need.

At Level Three, it's time to raise the stakes again, to give them what they don't even know they need.

This model represents the various perspectives you could leverage to deliver your next big innovation.

Your stakeholders typically focus towards the bottom left of the model. They know a lot about their business function and how it operates within the broader business. They also generally understand the context of their competitors and the market within which they operate.

But this is insufficient context to bring game-changing capability to your organisation. What's the difference? You.

By now, you've built a sizeable network of people outside the organisation through whom you've seen and heard lots of great ideas. You also have a team of unique and experienced professionals, an implementation partner who has case studies across multiple industries, and you're now intimately aware of the power of the platform on which you're sitting.

This is where the advice of Steve Jobs comes to bear. 'People don't know what they want until you show it to them. That's why I never rely on market research. Our task is to read things that are not yet on the page.'

It's time to bring these to the fore and lead.

Consider the guitar legend Jimi Hendrix. Other musicians had access to the same tone-altering tools and effects, but Hendrix was able to take them and create what Holly George-Warren of Rolling Stone referred to as a 'controlled, fluid vocabulary every bit as personal as the blues with which he began' (Romanowski, et al., 2001).

It's this ability to take the same tools that everyone has and use your creativity and experience to create something unique that is game-changing.

MATURITY LEVEL THREE
REALISE

This is where the advice of Steve Jobs comes to bear. 'People don't know what they want until you show it to them. That's why I never rely on market research. Our task is to read things that are not yet on the page.'

So, let's realise the full value of this platform. Launch your first major innovation, something the organisation would never have considered, something that will change everything for your business and, in turn, change the master-servant relationship to customer-advisor.

What does your big idea look like, and who will it serve?

How will you sell the benefits and build momentum for the change?

How will you earn your seat at the advisor's table?

BIG WINS FOR MINIMAL EFFORT

On occasion, the wins that will establish you as a leader and provide significant value won't necessarily take large amounts of effort, investment or time. During the peak of the 2020 coronavirus pandemic in New Zealand, Fisher & Paykel Appliances, like many other businesses, were receiving a growing volume of service calls that were increasingly challenging to service appropriately.

> On occasion, the wins that will establish you as a leader and provide significant value won't necessarily take large amounts of effort, investment or time.

When talking with their platform vendor, Salesforce, they heard that many organisations overseas had seen a dramatic uptake of customer interaction via the social chat channel – using Facebook Messenger to interact with consumers. Moreover, F&P already had access to

> Overnight the business had a valuable new capability live. One they didn't know they needed.

this capability on their platform, but it wasn't being leveraged.

As an innovative and agile leadership team, the EVP of marketing and customer experience took this insight and sprang into action. Within 48 hours, the service team at F&P had a fully operational social chat capability. This saw an almost immediate 30 per cent migration of phone traffic to asynchronous digital communication and a significant uptick in customer satisfaction. Overnight the business had a valuable new capability live. One they didn't know they needed.

Lucas's team had been beavering away in the background for several weeks, working on an innovation.

As usual, Lucas used the quarterly governance meeting to highlight wins for the quarter.

Off script, he then turned the conversation to his vision for the platform and the transformation of L&D. To illustrate the art of the possible, Lucas's team showcased their new initiative. Acme University: a learning community portal where leaders from across the organisation could develop and maintain their own e-learning modules and create certification tracks. Having secretly enlisted the L&D representative from Sales, Lucas was able to demonstrate how a Sales representative could upskill on the latest product changes without needing to come off the road and how all the progress could be tracked and tied back to the career and development plans. The head of Sales and the CFO quickly saw the commercial benefits. The Chief People Officer immediately realised the opportunity to lift the organisation's status in the 'employer of choice' rankings.

And the CIO was most interested in giving this capability to his vast software engineering teams, who had a solid but unstructured and unmeasured learning culture.

The exec team was stunned. Nobody saw this coming, but it was apparent that the new HRIS could add significant value to the organisation. Lucas had won their support.

PURPOSE

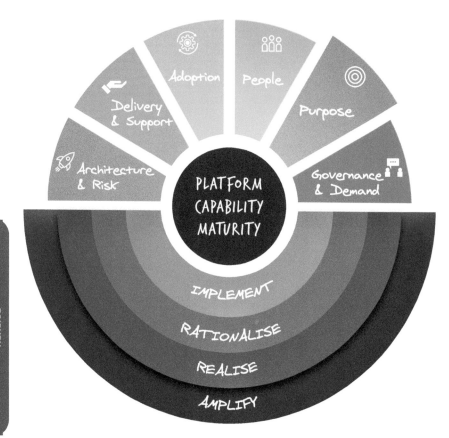

LOVE THE PROBLEM, NOT YOUR SOLUTION

Jennifer spotted an opportunity that everyone else missed – the sales teams gathered data from many sources and made their own interpretation of the information. For the most part, that meant they went looking for evidence to support a hunch that enabled them to create a sales pitch.

Jennifer wanted that to change. What if she could tap into those data sources, remove assumptions from the equation, and then visually put the data into the hands of the sales team with a clear call to action that they could execute immediately within the CRM?

The executive sponsor loved the idea, so he tasked the commercial managers with supporting Jennifer's team to produce the prototype.

Everyone in Jennifer's network was excited by the opportunity and leaned in. Analytics experts from the CRM vendor flew into town, their implementation partner took a few people off the bench to lend a hand at no charge, and the team revelled in the opportunity to show something amazing. Everything was heading in exactly the right direction.

TIME TO INNOVATE

If you genuinely want to realise the value of your platform, then, as discussed, it's time to innovate. What does that really mean? Well, it means testing a range of hypotheses and seeing what sticks.

The trap for young players is that we get attached to our ideas. We're so sure they're viable, that we're onto the right solution or that everything would be grand if they would just use it.

Don't get attached to your ideas.

ONLY A FEW IDEAS ARE GOOD IDEAS

What do penicillin and Scotchguard have in common? They were both discovered by accident as byproducts of attempting to achieve something else. Sir Alexander Fleming discovered penicillin when he threw out an experiment then noticed that mould in the contaminated Petri dish was dissolving the bacteria around it.

When you start innovating on your platform, you're moving into uncertain territory, and as this isn't an exact science, you should expect some ideas not to succeed.

If it's not working, then rather than burn more time and money trying to fit a square peg in a round hole, you are better to call it, take the learnings and apply them to your next big idea. Investing your energy into the next idea, while taking the lessons from the last, is a better use of everyone's time.

I met Ash Maurya, author of *Scaling Lean,* at a book signing a few years back. His inscription in the book makes this point perfectly: 'To Shane, love the problem, not your solution! Ash' (Maurya, 2016).

CHOOSING YOUR FAVOURITE CHILD

There are hundreds of great books on the topic of innovation* so I've decided to focus here on a technique I picked up for prioritising your ideas rather than executing on them.

 PRO-TIP

If you want a recommendation for a practical innovation book, check out *Innovators Playbook* by Nathan Baird (Baird, 2020).

The prioritisation process involves two steps.

First, put a case for each of your ideas on paper, then pitch them to your executive sponsor and see which one resonates best. You might ask why you'd go to all this effort when these are just ideas? I believe it forces you to consider whether an idea is really that good. When you pitch it, you want your exec sponsor to buy into you spending time on an idea, prepared that it might not work.

STEP ONE: GETTING YOUR IDEA DOWN

Have you heard of Amazon's customer-centred 'working backwards' process? Essentially it proposes that you start with the end in mind and work backward. Their process involves writing a press release as if you'd just launched the innovation. If you've never worked in media or marketing and thus never penned a press release, never fear. Ian McAllister, a Director at Amazon, shared the process on Quora https://www.quora.com/What-is-Amazons-approach-to-product-development-and-product-management.

In the post, McAllister shared an example outline. Since then, several templates have appeared online. Most of them are good and follow the same standard format, but because they focus on a product and not a platform, I think they fall short on suitability for platform teams.

They seem to miss measurable outcomes, the metrics that we'll use to prove if the innovation meets the targeted need. (Otherwise, how will you know to let it go?) And they don't recognise that platform teams often need to collaborate with other teams and departments to deliver value.

Here's my interpretation of Amazon's Press Release approach to customer-centric innovations.

1. Heading: Name the product you just shipped; something punchy that your target end-user or customer will understand.

2. Subheading: Describe the stakeholder group and the benefit to them. Keep it to one sentence.

3. Summary: Give a summary of the innovation and its benefits. This should be a statement, not a feature list, for example, 'Ensures no application for open roles is missed, regardless of the channel by which it was submitted'. It can be more than one sentence but keep it brief. Write it assuming that the reader won't read any further.

4. Problem: Describe the problem your innovation solves. How does it make your stakeholder more successful? What can users now do better or more efficiently?

5. Solution: Describe how your innovation solves the problem AND how you know. This is one of the gaps I talked about earlier. If you run the experiment, how will you know, with data, whether it was successful? What new behaviour can you measure that proves it meets the need? Another way to think about this might be, 'If we launch this, what will the user do differently from today?'

6. Quote from your sponsor: A spokesperson's quote describing why the team took on this challenge and how it improved the user experience. Include here what it took in terms of collaboration to get the job done and what challenges you overcame to make the innovation successful. Did you have to work across geographies? Were there legal implications to consider?

7. How to get started: Describe how easy it is to adopt.

8. Customer quote: Share a quote that provides a stakeholder view of how this product made them successful or made something easier. Be sure to note the type of user and their role. Include how the innovation fits into their day-to-day and how their experience has improved. Avoid feature specifics and go for aspirational statements like 'increased commission' or 'more time with family'.

9. Closing and call to action: Wrap up your case and direct the reader on what to do next. Should they download an app or register their interest on a URL?

Other thoughts:

Write this so your Grandma could understand. It shouldn't be a specification for the design; remember, a press release is a marketing tool.

Keep it brief. If you want to take your stakeholder through a few of these, keep them to a maximum page and a half length.

> Keep it brief. If you want to take your stakeholder through a few of these, keep them to a maximum page and a half length.

STEP TWO: DECIDING WHICH HORSE TO BACK

Once you have thought deeply about your best ideas and how you might pull them together, it's time to pitch the ideas. At first, do this with your team to ensure there are no obvious gaps and practice driving home the benefits. Then move to your executive sponsor or key stakeholders. Which idea gets them most excited?

> Once you have thought deeply about your best ideas and how you might pull them together, it's time to pitch the ideas.

The benefit of this approach is that it opens up your innovation agenda to ensure executive support and sets you up as a thought leader, thus changing your status from service provider to an advisor.

For the most part, Jennifer's analytics pilot went well. Using the analytics capability, the team build a functional sales console with insights derived from the CRM and finance system data that showed much promise. The system was providing actionable insights, and the executive stakeholder was impressed. But something was missing.

The key information that tied consumer website behaviour back to advertising customer data was built and maintained by Sales operations. It was a complex database built over several years and was guarded closely by that team.

Jennifer had anticipated that either the operations team would immediately see and adopt the benefits of the new tooling capabilities, or she would simply plug the raw source data into the new tools and effectively make their system redundant.

She misread the play on both counts. The logic that tied all the source data together and was critical to making the new tools had taken years to develop. The operations team had a strong affinity with their existing tooling and little interest in learning or taking on a new toolset regardless of potential benefits. They had also just invested heavily in training and signed a multi-year renewal for their expensive data visualisation technology. Without the support and co-operation of Sales operations, this innovation would never provide value.

Jennifer was still convinced, but business conditions didn't support its success. As a compromise, Jennifer collaborated to embed the operations teams visualisation tooling into the CRM. That meant the sales team no longer had to go to a separate system to see their data which was, at least, a marginal win. Jennifer and the team then turned their attention to the next big innovation.

PURPOSE

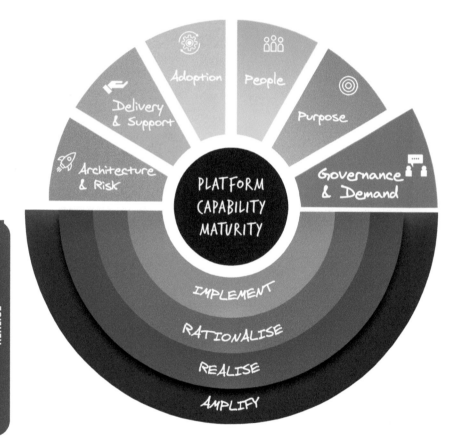

MATURITY LEVEL THREE
REALISE

PRIORITISING WITH DATA

As the business continued its digital transformation, the CIO was laser-focused on delivering the e-commerce platform and mobile experience. 'The new app is the primary focus for the board; anything the digital team needs to support getting the next three releases live is your number one priority Deepika. We have some pretty aggressive revenue numbers to hit, and the board is expecting this to land. Clear?'

Despite valiant attempts, Deepika could not convince the CIO that they needed to focus on other related work.

During the initial platform implementation, the platform team had built some fairly sophisticated monitoring and alerting for the enterprise systems. The digital team now adopted these tools as the organisational standard to monitor web security and e-commerce availability. As the web capabilities and traffic volumes increased, the system provided exceptional value in terms of resource demand forecasting.

There was, however, one issue. The monitoring tooling was implemented well before the digital transformation strategy. The vendor who provided the monitoring software was then a new player in the market and keen to get a well-known logo on their client list. Deepika's predecessor had negotiated a great deal with unlimited volume and a fixed price for three years. But the environment had changed. The vendor was now a significantly successful player in the market, and the volume of data passing through the system, generated by the new digital volumes, was significantly more than the original estimates. There were still twelve months until the renewal, but Deepika thought the organisation was sitting on a ticking cost bomb.

UNDERSTANDING VALUE AND URGENCY

Have you found it challenging to justify business cases that don't have a revenue or growth number attached to them? Many platform owners tell me that the initiatives that really should be done but can't be honestly tied to a revenue metric just get deprioritised. Getting funding becomes even more difficult when your platform is not directly attached to revenue-generating activities such as sales and marketing. Some platform owners will play the game of loading a bunch of artificial costs into a revenue-generating business case, so they have some buffer to tackle these jobs under the radar. For example, you can't justify rebuilding the unsupported but functional two-factor authentication capability in your ITSM tool, but the business is investing in an e-commerce refresh, so you create a tenuous link to that project. How would you genuinely justify this work?

> Many platform owners tell me that the initiatives that really should be done but can't be honestly tied to a revenue metric just get deprioritised.

Then there's the challenge of prioritising. Even if you find a way to quantify the cost-benefit of the non-revenue generating capability, how will you decide which projects should be prioritised?

In essence, the challenge for platform owners is quantifying value and urgency. The answer is to measure the cost of delay.

JUSTIFYING AND PRIORITISING INVESTMENTS

Let's say your executive stakeholder has two potential projects in front of her.

One delivers a new e-commerce capability that is expected to increase sales by $1m over twelve months.

The second replaces a piece of legacy technology that will save $80,000 per month.

If we assume both projects cost the same to deliver, then on the surface, they give us roughly the same return. But the first provides a new customer capability in the market which maintains our competitive edge. Which way do you think they'll go?

Now let's consider prioritisation at the platform team level.

At Maturity Level Three, your platform team will be trusted to prioritise their work. However, most average platform teams (those who never get past Level Three Maturity) aren't particularly scientific about how they prioritise. It's mostly gut feeling, first in/first out, do the most interesting work first or oil the squeaky wheel. It's estimated that 85 per cent of product developers do not know the cost of delay for the products they are working on. If you independently asked people working on the same product about those costs, their answers will vary by 50 to 1 (Andreasson, 2011)

GET SCIENTIFIC

Conversely, a high performing platform capability on a trajectory to amplify value is more scientific in its prioritisation. As demonstrated, understanding the cost of not doing something is arguably more important than knowing the cost of doing something.

> Sometimes it's difficult to quantify the cost of delay. Often value won't be easy to estimate, and the team will believe a simple dollar figure can't be applied to an initiative.

Sometimes it's difficult to quantify the cost of delay. Often value won't be easy to estimate, and the team will believe a simple dollar figure can't be applied to an initiative. In response, I often quote Douglas Hubbard's book, *How to Measure Anything*, where he describes the belief that some things are immeasurable as 'sand in the gears of the entire economy'. He asserts that 'Any important decision-maker could benefit from learning that anything they really need to know is measurable' (Hubbard, 2014).

> I believe the key to improving the accuracy of estimates is to systematically strengthen our estimation over time. That starts with addressing the Achilles heel of estimation – assumptions.

The challenge with estimation is that, like all platform development, it is full of risk and unknowns that breed uncertainty; yet we need certainty to make good business decisions. That means better estimates.

Of course, the goal is accuracy, which sounds like an oxymoron when we've just acknowledged this is all a big guess. I believe the key to improving the accuracy of estimates is to systematically strengthen our estimation over time. That starts with addressing the Achilles heel of estimation – assumptions.

So how do we do that? Transparency and critique. Estimation accuracy will increase when your assumptions are exposed.

The key to assumption transparency is twofold:

1. Apply probability to your assumptions

2. Be explicit in your assumptions.

Making them visible allows assumptions to be openly scrutinised and challenged. Importantly instilling a culture of exposing assumptions stops the system from being gamed with blatant false numbers to drive an agenda. A regular cadence of prioritisation sessions where ideas and projects are respectfully challenged to collectively refine the estimates, will systematically improve the quality of estimates over time. You're playing the long game here; learning to better estimate with improved accuracy is a skill that will exponentially improve value.

> You're playing the long game here; learning to better estimate with improved accuracy is a skill that will exponentially improve value.

Let's say we've now developed a continually improving system of accurate estimation and are confident in our ability to calculate a reasonable cost of delay. How do we use it?

There's a wealth of literature on Weighted Shortest Job First (WSJF), so I won't go into detail here. That said, I've found that executives who are comfortable with financials seem to respond well to the Cost of Delay Divided by Duration (CD3) variant. CD3 also works well with teams with fixed capacity and often forces a conversation about breaking initiatives down into smaller pieces of work that can be delivered incrementally. Agility anyone?

To demonstrate how you might use the cost of delay to encourage better decision-making within your organisation, let's revisit our executive stakeholder presented with an e-commerce project and a legacy tech refresh.

Our e-commerce proposal is estimated to take twelve months to deliver.

GOVERNANCE & ADOPTION

Conversely, our platform refresh is mostly a turn-key solution that will take your team six weeks to implement.

Rather than 'these cost the same, but one has a cool new capability attached', your stakeholder is now presented with a very different proposal – an estimated $1m revenue over twenty-four months versus a $1.8m saving over the same period. It mightn't win, but the system replacement just got a whole lot more enticing. Money talks.

In an article in Lean Magazine, Don Reinertsen commented that 'management always has surplus of good ideas to spend money on. When we package our choices within an economic framework we enable management to choose between these ideas quickly and correctly' (Andreasson, 2010).

THE PAYOFF

MATURITY LEVEL THREE
REALISE

Applying a scientific approach to your platform development might initially be a challenge, but it will have a demonstrable impact on your ability to realise more value for your organisation.

In his book *The Principles of Product Development Flow*, Reinertsen asserts that this methodology enables companies to achieve five to ten times improvement in product development speed, quality and efficiency (Reinertsen, 2009).

Getting these types of concepts right in your approach to executive and team prioritisation and decision-making is

> Applying a scientific approach to your platform development might initially be a challenge, but it will have a demonstrable impact on your ability to realise more value for your organisation.

the difference between good and great, the stepping stone to Level Four Maturity.

Deepika convinced her finance business partner to help her model the problem. Based on volumes generated after each mobile app release and the subsequent marketing activity, the finance BP forecast that by renewal time in twelve months, the system would be processing upwards of 50x the volumes of data it had been when the first contract was penned. Moreover, the monitoring product was now a market leader and approaching an IPO, so revenue per customer was crucial, and a significant discount was unlikely. That meant, even with an ambitious 40 per cent discount on the public rate card, the organisation would be up for a 20 per cent price increase. That per cent cost increase on 50x usage presented a dire financial situation. Granted, it was twelve months away, but nobody was expecting this cost, and it would erode most of the profit generated from the new e-commerce platform.

When presented with the cost of delay, the business case was obvious. Deepika was able to bring on two additional resources to work with the vendor and the digital teams to refactor how the solution was implemented. While the subsequent two releases were slightly delayed, the impact on the cost for the renewal was minimised.

GOVERNANCE & ADOPTION

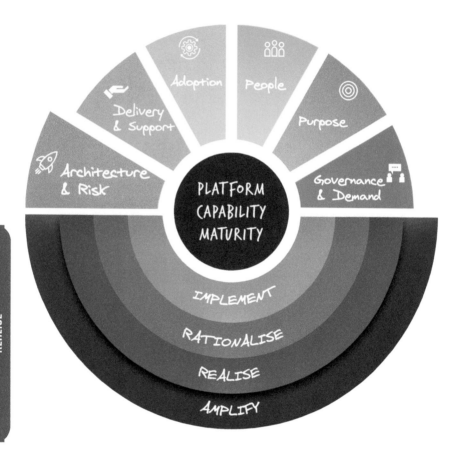

PLATFORMS ARE RARELY ISLANDS

LIKE YOUR BUSINESS, YOUR PLATFORM DOESN'T OPERATE IN A VACUUM

Stop for a second and think about an end-to-end value stream in your organisation. In an HR context, that might be the recruitment journey – from identifying the need for a new role and seeking approval through the candidate hiring journey and onboarding. In a sales context, it might be prospecting for leads through sales, provisioning and collection of cash.

Have you got one? Ok, good. If you were to write that up on a whiteboard, then overlay the individuals and teams involved, plus all the technology solutions that serve those people, how many would there be? In almost all cases, more than one, and that means we need to start looking beyond our patch to truly unlock business value across the organisation. This is where enterprise architecture fits in.

> When it comes time to make investments to support those objectives, supported by multiple technologies, how will you coordinate the changes so that everyone is marching in the same direction with a clear understanding of each part of the challenge?

SEEING THE FOREST FOR THE TREES

Now let's take things up to a macro level. What is your organisation's purpose or mission? What business objectives support that mission? When it comes time to make investments to support those objectives, supported by multiple technologies, how will you coordinate the changes so that everyone is marching in the same direction with a clear understanding of each part of the challenge? We don't want to create silos, bottlenecks, or blindly march in the wrong direction.

Importantly, if your platform capability is to emerge from Level Three into amplifying value, you won't be able to do it in isolation.

DON'T OVERCOOK IT!

First of all, please don't run down the rabbit hole of standing up an 'Enterprise Architecture project'. Not only is it a distraction, but WhiteCloudSoftware estimates that 66 per cent of all EA initiatives fail. You might not need the specific role of an enterprise architect, but you're looking for someone with the aptitude and time to look more broadly across the tech landscape (rather than deep into one platform) and help align the multiple technology roadmaps with the business objectives. Be careful about who you choose and how you position the role. With the democratisation of IT and the proliferation of SaaS applications implemented by business units rather than a central technology function, the traditional role of enterprise architect needs to evolve lest it becomes a barrier to innovation and a useless governance bottleneck.

> First of all, please don't run down the rabbit hole of standing up an 'Enterprise Architecture project'. Not only is it a distraction, but WhiteCloudSoftware estimates that 66 per cent of all EA initiatives fail.

So assuming we're on the same page and you see the value, what now?

MATURITY LEVEL THREE
REALISE

I think the process looks something like this:

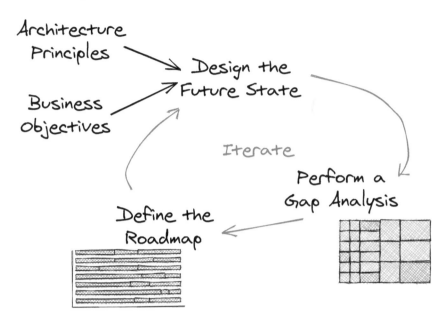

1. Define your architecture principles

2. Design the future state

3. Perform a gap analysis

4. Define the roadmap(s)

Then return to step two and iterate, taking into account any learnings from platform delivery and changes to business objectives.

WHAT DO YOU MEAN BY ARCHITECTURE PRINCIPLES?

These are a set of principles that apply to the broader technology environment against which all platform owners must align. If the business objective was to drive a car from Sydney to Brisbane, then the principles would be the road rules. The team at Workday shared their architecture principles a couple of years back, and I think they're a good representation to give you an idea of what yours might look like.

Workday Enterprise Architecture Guiding Principles

Business ↑	Customer Satisfaction	Customer Satisfaction is paramount (>95%)
	High Touch Support	Workday prides itself in providing a high touch support and is vital for customer satisfaction
	Simplified Experience	The experience should be simple for workday employees, customers and partners
	Customer Success	Genuine care for making customers successful is a key differentiator
	Community	Workday encourages all their customers to become an active participant in the community
	Trust	Security, transparency and accountability. Protecting customer's sensitive data is critical
	Agile & Simplicity	Simplified Architecture & Agile delivery to align with business agility and growth
Technology ↓	Data	Unleash the power of data by sharing relevant data across the organisation

SO WE HAVE OUR PRINCIPLES, NOW WHAT?

I'll assume the concepts of defining the future state, performing a gap analysis and defining roadmaps are self-evident. However, the guidance here is to keep it lightweight and iterative so the business can continue to innovate. It also means the delivery teams can continue to provide value, avoiding analysis paralysis and wasted effort on extensive detailed artefacts nobody will refer to and are largely obsolete soon after they've been developed.

STILL NOT CONVINCED?

In 2014 News Corp Australia identified an opportunity to provide tailored omni-channel digital marketing services to SMB customers. The enterprise architect, working with various platform teams, designed an end-to-end solution that enabled bundling of News

Corp's own digital products with other digital advertising platform products to deliver performance marketing campaigns at scale. The platforms that supported selling and provisioning those services were delivered iteratively over several years as the business scaled. Five years later, News Xtend had an estimated revenue of AU$24m and then partnered with a media company in Singapore to bring the offer to a new geographical market (Zoominfo, n.d.). Oh, and for what it's worth, that same enterprise architect was snapped up for a great role inside Salesforce shortly after putting that plan together.

ARCHITECTURE & RISK

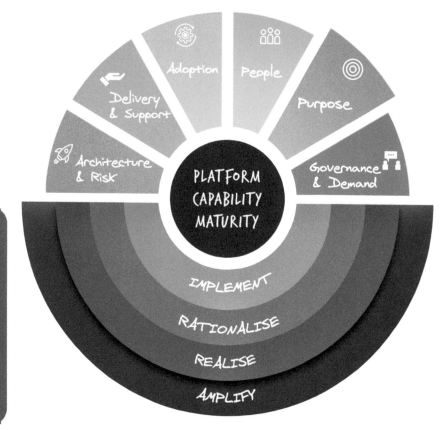

TAKING STOCK

CONSIDERING AMPLIFICATION? PAUSE FOR THOUGHT.

Sustainably operating at the 'Realise' level of maturity is a rewarding long-term strategy that provides a significant return for the organisation. After at least twelve months at this level, it is timely to consider the longer-term ambitions for the platform in the organisation.

Have the original strategic goals of the platform been achieved?

On the current trajectory, are we positioned to continue to deliver sustainable value?

Are we ready to dial it up and really amplify value?

The diagram below demonstrates the Level 3/4 reflection point.

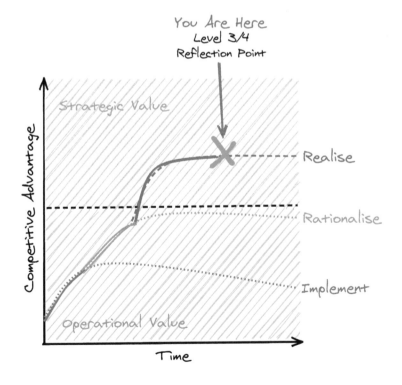

WHY NOW?

Moving to Maturity Level Four and truly amplifying value requires dialling up the momentum. Turning a 5x return to 10x return on an enterprise platform is something very few organisations achieve. It will require significant stakeholder support and shifts in capability across all six domains. Without taking stock of the successes to date, the current trajectory and influencing factors, it will be difficult to know where to focus, and a whole lot of effort could be burned for little amplification.

AMPLIFYING SIGNAL WITHOUT NOISE

The reflection point process contains five steps:

1. Collate: Gather the artefacts required for the review

2. Review: Examine the current platform against the original business case and platform vision

3. Consider: Look at current environmental factors

4. Decide: Make the call to sustain or amplify

5. Design: Create a new vision and roadmap

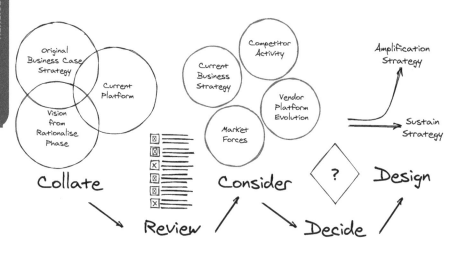

1. Collate

When did you last take a look at the original platform implementation business case? I imagine not for some time. Before considering dialling up the effort, it would be useful to re-examine the strategic intent that drove the decision to implement the solution. In many cases, this will be before your time, and there might not be anyone left in the team who was around for the initial implementation. A trip down memory lane will provide some interesting reflection.

Next, reflect on the vision set for the platform at the beginning of the rationalise stage shortly after the implementation. You had big plans, and you're realising great value. How much of that was planned, and how much was luck?

2. Review

Now take a look at the current state of the platform and the capabilities delivered and compare them to the implementation and rationalisation stage strategies.

Did/does the platform meet the original strategic objectives of the organisation? Are those objectives still valid? What's changed?

Have you achieved the transformational vision for the organisation you set out to achieve? What successes did you have? What got in the way?

3. Consider

The world doesn't stand still while you're busy building a world-class platform capability. Over time, the organisation's leadership will change, market forces and competitor behaviour will evolve, and possibly with that comes some new strategic direction. Further, your platform vendor will continue to invest heavily in R&D and M&A to bring new capabilities for your consideration.

How do these influences change your vision for the platform?

PURPOSE

What level of appetite is there for further investment and continued transformation in the organisation?

Can you use the platform to fundamentally enhance the business strategy by providing an amplified technology-driven competitive advantage?

4. Decide

It's time to make the call.

Is the platform in a position to provide amplified levels of return? If not, how close?

Are the market conditions such that you could leverage this platform for a significant advantage over your competitors?

Are your business's strategic objectives screaming out for a platform solution?

Are your technology teams ready to take cross-platform enterprise architecture and delivery to the next level?

Is your business leadership ready to be technology-led?

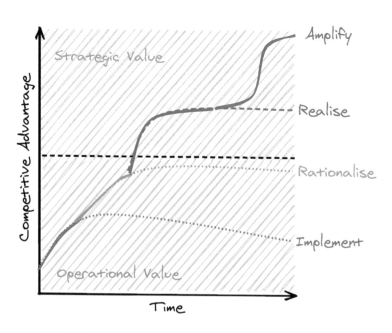

If not, that's ok. Perhaps it's just not now rather than never. You can continue delivering exceptional value at Level Three – after all, few organisations take the leap to Level Four. Consider revisiting this decision in twelve months.

SO YOU'VE DECIDED TO AMPLIFY

Let's extend the model because here's where the rubber really hits the road.

When Telstra, one of Australia's largest telcos, decided to amplify value with their platform, they kicked off their T22 Strategy. At the time, Nevash Pillay, Global Partner Sales Executive, stated, 'I think the future success of any company, including Telstra, is to be ahead of the game and serve our customers brilliantly'. This meant empowering collaboration from all corners of the organisation, including their partners, with a vision to radically simplify its products, eliminate customer pain points and create all-digital experiences.

Telstra leveraged their Salesforce investment and consolidated all their customer insights onto a single platform. They followed by providing capabilities for partners to interact directly with the platform. Mirko Gropp, Digital Enablement Principal, Telstra Enterprise, commented, 'For the first time, we have everybody collaborating on the same platform for the benefit of our customers... We're able to focus on the things that matter'. Pillay reflected, 'Working with Salesforce and digitising our business has enabled us to work seamlessly with our partners and customers and accelerate our pace of change. It's made it easy for all of us to move along the journey of creating business success.'

Twelve months after delivering T22, NPS within Telstra has increased eighty points, and the company's sales pipeline increased 27 per cent. Still, Telstra believes their journey is not over (Salesforce, 2021), (Crozier, 2019).

PURPOSE

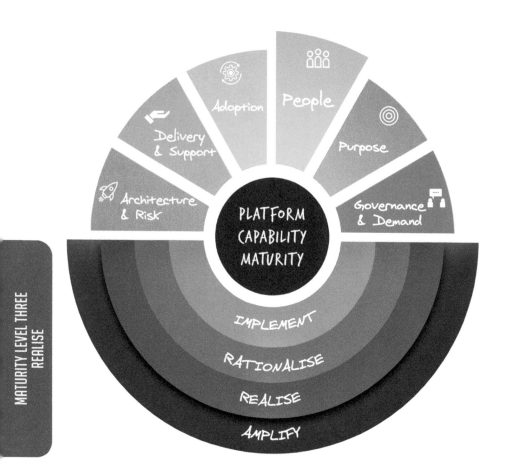

MATURITY LEVEL THREE
REALISE

PLATFORM CAPABILITY MATURITY

People
Adoption
Delivery & Support
Architecture & Risk
Purpose
Governance & Demand

IMPLEMENT
RATIONALISE
REALISE
AMPLIFY

SUSTAINING HIGH PERFORMANCE

Over three year, Lucas and his platform team had progressively transformed Learning & Development, talent acquisition and remuneration across APAC, EMEA and the Americas. Lucas had a well-earned seat at the global People & Culture leadership table.

At the P&C end of year celebration, Lucas managed to chat with the Chief People Officer.

'I'm really enjoying working on your team Tim,' began Lucas, 'and I've been thinking that given the success we've achieved and recognising my background in HR, I'd be keen to formalise my position in your leadership team in a capacity that represents the value I bring to the organisation being greater than platform owner.'

'Lucas, there's no doubt that you've delivered some great work and built some outstanding relationships across the organisation. You should be exceptionally proud. We take comfort in knowing that this capability you've built is in safe hands with you at the helm. The truth is, you're indispensable to this organisation, and we need you and your team to keep doing what you do best, so we can sweat the asset'.

It was hardly the support Lucas was looking for. He prided himself in being indispensable, but where to from here? Although there was never a shortage of continuous improvement work, the business showed no appetite to take it to the next level.

Where did this leave the platform team, including Lucas, in terms of attracting and retaining talent?

REALISING VALUE SUSTAINABLY

Up to this point, you've probably been so busy building your platform capability and ramping up the value that you've not had time to think about what it takes to make this sustainable. That's fair – there have been more important things to consider.

However, sustaining Level Three or launching to Level Four both have a small challenge that we need to address. How sustainably structured is the team?

What do I mean by sustainably structured? Well, I'm talking about two things:

1. Your people: Do they have career paths that offer ongoing opportunity and challenge?

2. You: Are you indispensable?

CAPABILITY SUSTAINABILITY

Let's start with you? What is your personal brand within the organisation? Are you, for example, Ms Workday, Mr Salesforce or Mx ServiceNow? That's not necessarily a bad thing, but it might be a little limiting if you want to be an amplifier. Moving the capability to Level Four requires the platform owner to take on a strategic role within the organisation. That means, for example, accountability for one or many HR, Technology or Sales and Marketing functions. At Level Four, it's no longer just about the platform but being accountable for a strategic business capability.

If you're known for being the (insert product name) person, then chances are you're likely to be stuck there. The traits that got you to this position were being the expert, putting in the hard yards, juggling everything, having all the answers. Your promotions have primarily been a reward in recognition of it all. You're indispensable because you're the go-to person, which probably means you're doing too much work and not spending enough time on strategic thinking. Would you believe that some CEOs spend as little as one per cent of their time on the top strategic priorities, distracted, instead, by operational issues (Jolly, 2011). That's not uncommon, just not helpful.

Now here's the hard truth. Being indispensable is both a fallacy and a curse.

Let's address the fallacy. No matter what you tell yourself, if you were somehow to disappear off the radar tomorrow and be totally out of contact for several months, the people around you would just figure it out – the business wouldn't stop. Surely someone critical in your team left, probably when the implementation was complete, and the partner rolled off. Did the place grind to a halt? No. Nobody is indispensable. To quote the former French President, Charles de Gaulle, 'The graveyards are full of indispensable men'.

Being indispensable can be a curse. If you're just too good at what you do, the executive team couldn't possibly afford to move you to another broader role; who would fill your shoes? And how will you progress your career if you're indispensable?

Then there's your team. As the capability matures, the tenure of your key people increases with it. While team members love the organisation and team culture and revel in transformational innovation, they'll still look for career advancement. How will you keep your key talent, bring in fresh blood and sustain your high performance without a solid plan?

MAKE YOURSELF REDUNDANT

Embrace the principle to make yourself redundant. Across twenty years in the corporate world, I've seen very successful executives who have never held a single role for longer than two years. The focus on setting up high performing teams and succession plans meant the ability to move rapidly between new opportunities, learning and experiences. This concept might feel awkward or counter-intuitive, but if you want to progress your career and provide opportunities for your team, you have to face the prospect that you can't stay in your current role forever.

So you have two jobs here to set your team up for sustainability.

> It can be uncomfortable to let go and allow your successor to pick up the skills you feel are critical.

1. Develop your successor(s)

2. Be deliberate and overt about career paths, development and opportunities.

Develop your successor

It can be uncomfortable to let go and allow your successor to pick up the skills you feel are critical. So I've come up with an easy model to help you both through the journey.

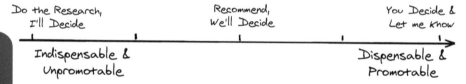

As the model suggests, the idea is to move from 'I'll decide' over to 'Let me know'. This is a fairly simple three step process.

Step One: At every important decision, ask your 2IC to gather the information necessary to make the decision. This is an excellent first step because it will free up your time to work on more strategic matters but still leave you with a sense of control over the decision. It also means you're guiding your 2IC in understanding the inputs you feel are important to the decision-making process.

Step Two: When they've got the hang of soliciting the appropriate information for making decisions, ask them to recommend a decision. This will give you a sense of which inputs they favour and which assumptions they rely on. Use this phase to coach them through making the right decisions.

Step Three: Hand over decisions and ask to be kept informed. If the proverbial hits the fan, then deal with the consequences and let them learn. By this point, you'll be focussed on more important things, such as career opportunities for your team and positioning yourself for your next opportunity.

Career paths, development and opportunities

If the size of your team is growing in line with business growth and value of the platform, then you'll be able to slice the team into specialisations and create leadership roles. I'll assume you have a nice balance of internal promotion and fresh blood entering the team.

If the platform is no longer in a growth phase but rather an operation run scenario, career pathing can be a little more difficult. However, regardless of role (including yours) and whether you're in growth or operations, I think there are four career trajectories you can discuss with your people that are honest, achievable and motivational. I've illustrated these below:

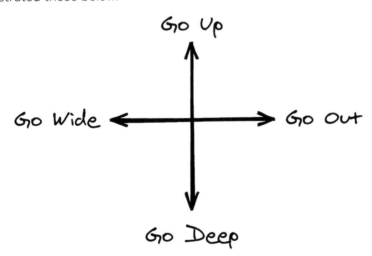

Go Up: This is fairly self-explanatory – get promoted. But in a team that isn't growing, that's often easier said than done.

Go Wide: Stretch their expertise into other areas. If they're an expert in one vertical of the business, then learn another. If they're across one part of the technology, learn about another. Increase your value and motivation through new learning.

Go Deep: Hyper-specialise. If you're a developer, for example, push yourself to become a domain architect. Get formally trained and certified.

Go out: Move on to something outside the team or organisation. Remember our archetypes? Sometimes you can't keep the players. Often, this isn't seen as an option or is uncomfortable to discuss, but it shouldn't be in a psychologically safe, high-performing team. I simply couldn't give some of the best people I've ever worked with what they desired within their team or organisation. So we had a sensible adult conversation, put together a development plan that meant the organisation got the benefit of their service for a while and simultaneously set them up for securing their preferred next opportunity. You never know, things change, and you might get them back one day with a whole bunch of new skills and experience.

CREATING ROLES ISN'T NECESSARILY THE ANSWER

I recently worked with a client who has a mature capability. They continue to innovate, and although the work is enjoyable, the team was starting to wonder about its career opportunities. This is particularly a problem for functional consultants heavily tied to the platform technology but who aren't software developers. It means their ability to transition into other parts of the organisation or climb the IT engineering ranks is limited.

It seemed logical (so the leadership thought) that a new senior role within the functional ranks; would give the already senior team a leadership role to aspire to. So a lead role was created.

Can you guess what happened? Overnight, four mildly despondent senior people became one happy and three disgruntled people – the complete opposite of the desired outcome.

Fortunately, this team has an experienced leader, and the organisation has well-established processes for employee feedback and career development. Those who missed out were kindly made aware of the skills needed to develop to move to their next opportunity. One began skilling up from deep technical expertise toward a future people leadership role. Another pursued a more specialist technical role. It worked out ok for them but creating a single desirable role in a less mature organisation could easily spell disaster.

Lucas spent some time considering his options, cognisant that he didn't want to remain the platform owner forever. After a few years abroad, he decided that it was time for him and his family to return to Australia.

Lucas and his leadership team set about reviewing the delivery team and governance structures to enable career progression and learning opportunities while sustainably realising value from the platform. Lucas spent the next six months progressively handing over operational leadership for the platform to Evy, his now second in charge, who had a great passion for the platform. Lucas considered that Evy was, in many respects, more capable than himself.

Lucas went on to start a boutique advisory consultancy and specialises in supporting organisations to get HRIS platform sponsorship and adoption right.

PEOPLE

	Maturity	$ROI	Effort : Return
Strategic Value ↑	~~Amplify~~	x 10	1 : ~~20~~
	Realise	x 5	1 : 10
	Tipping Point		
Operational Value ↑	Rationalise	x 1	1 : 1
	Implement	x 0.5	2 : 1

MATURITY LEVEL FOUR

AMPLIFY

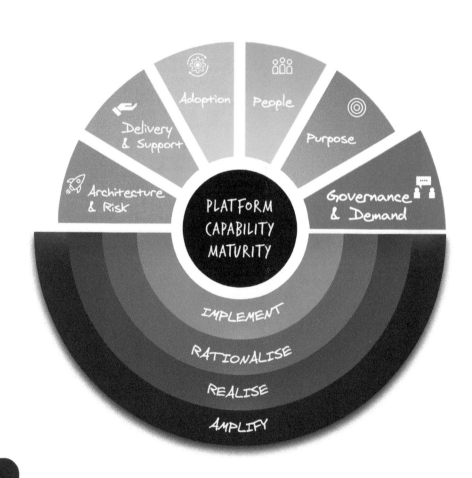

Platform Capability Maturity

- Adoption
- People
- Delivery & Support
- Purpose
- Architecture & Risk
- Governance & Demand

IMPLEMENT
RATIONALISE
REALISE
AMPLIFY

THE PILOT'S CHAIR

FLIPPING THE DYNAMIC

At the beginning of Maturity Level Three, the goal was to be an innovative and cost-effective supplier to the business. Working through Level Three towards Level Four, you spent significant effort leveraging your platform, team and networks to bring new opportunities to life and prove the value of the platform.

But remember, what you've built is more than a technology platform. It is a strategic capability around a platform. With that capability now proven, amplification of value comes from taking it to the next level, thus transcending the platform and enabling the entire business to leverage it to become more agile, innovative and digital-focused. As illustrated below, that begins by flipping the dynamic, starting with a technology-led (rather than tech-enabled) digital strategy and business agility.

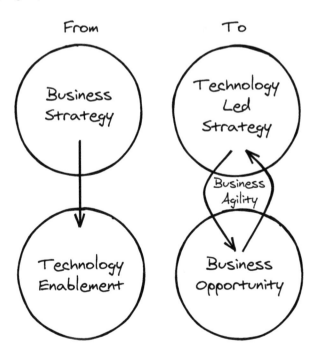

DISRUPTION IS EVERYWHERE AND INCREASING

In the late 1950s, the average age of companies on the S&P 500 was sixty-one years. By 2020 that had dropped to twenty-two years. When you consider the threat of global tech companies looking for opportunities, nimble digital start-ups eager to chip away at the establishment and the impact on markets and consumers of global pandemics, disruption is a constant, and businesses need to continue to evolve and innovate to survive. This evolution is, almost entirely, digital first.

> It's time to take the lead, to inform and shape the business strategy rather than simply enable it.

As far back as 2007, research published by Global Chief Strategist at IBM Saul J. Berman found that businesses making technology a key input to their strategy achieved a significant competitive advantage. We saw this play out during the 2007-2008 global financial crisis. Companies able to move quickly and decisively did best coming out of recession. By 2016, those same companies had performed up to 150 percentage points better than their competitors.

Your capability is built to deal with uncertainty and is likely far more nimble than many other parts of your business. It's time to take the lead, to inform and shape the business strategy rather than simply enable it.

TECHNOLOGY-LED STRATEGY

Berman's research provided six core principles for technology-driven strategy innovators that still hold true today (Berman 2007).

1. Consider technology a core input

2. Revisit strategy and technology context regularly

3. Uniquely manage emerging business opportunities

4. Plan for disruptions

5. Manage for today's and tomorrow's context

6. Focus technology on the customers' priorities.

Let's consider Berman's principles one and two. At Level Three, we discussed how to leverage your network, vendors and partners to understand the art of the possible in terms of industry trends and opportunities to leverage technology. It stands to reason to continue this as a core input to the strategy and regularly revisit it.

Principle three speaks to emerging business opportunities. One of the most significant contributions platforms make in digital strategy is enabling ecosystems, where a network of digital partnerships can deliver products and services.

For example, in real estate, agents no longer just compete with the agent down the street when managing investment property because digital startups create solutions that enable more players to make headway in that space. A response might be an ecosystem play that would see real estate businesses partnering with insurance and maintenance service providers to create a complementary ecosystem of services to bring value to landlords, providing turn-key management and income certainty. This type of ecosystem play is already happening on a grand scale in some markets.

Take the case of grocery stores in the United States that face challenges as Amazon devastates their traditional business model following the acquisition of Whole Foods. McKinsey research suggests that digital ecosystems will account for more than US$60 trillion in revenues by 2025 or more than 30 per cent of global corporate revenues (McKinsey & Company, 2020).

GOVERNANCE & DEMAND

> 'If there's one thing that's certain in business, it's uncertainty.'

Principles four and five speak to digital disruption, managing for future context and uncertainty.

As Dr Stephen Covey wrote, 'If there's one thing that's certain in business, it's uncertainty' (Stephen R. Covey, 2009).

The value your capability brings to manage uncertainty is an agile mindset and ways of working by unlocking the power of an operating model that centres on objectives and not tasks. It requires embracing a culture of experimentation, empowerment and feedback. One of the best demonstrators of an agile business mindset at work is Amazon, which, among other things, deliberately hires big-thinkers with a beginner's mindset, are eager to learn and can deliver results. Their culture of innovation, comfort with uncertainty and preparedness for disruption enabled them to, for example, bring their one-hour delivery service 'Prime Now' from concept to launch in 111 days (Galetti, 2020).

In terms of impact, principle six, focusing technology on customer priorities, is perhaps the most significant that your platform capability mindset can bring. Leveraging your platform capability and understanding where new customer value will come from enables the creation of new technology-led business models for traditional products or services.

Consider the market shift to digital retailing and services that resulted from the 2020 coronavirus pandemic. Research suggests that entire consumer groups tried digital products for the first time. By August 2020, digital health products had achieved 10 per cent market penetration. Customer behaviour research in B2B found that digital interaction became twice as important as traditional channels in the same period (Gavin, et al., 2020).

TECHNOLOGY-LED MASTERS

Do you need more proof that a tech-led strategy is the way to amplify value? Let's think about some globally recognised companies that are technology-led and how they demonstrated Berman's principles to change the game. Tesla, Airbnb, eBay and Uber are classic examples of tech-led organisations that have achieved remarkable success, broken the rules of scale and introduced totally new business models. They achieved this by considering technology as their core input, focussing their technology on customers' priorities, uniquely managing emerging business opportunities and constantly revisiting their strategies.

TRANSCENDING THE PLATFORM

Over seven years, the Salesforce platform capability at Fisher & Paykel Appliances grew from a Maturity Level One Marketing Cloud implementation to Maturity Level Four entire platform play that encompasses all aspects of the customer journey. During this time, it delivered significant value and proved itself able to respond to business needs or market disruption with exceptional agility. In early 2021, the executive leadership team recognised the value this customer-obsessed agility brought to the business. They decided the same level of flexibility was required in marketing and customer experience and across all technology, so Rudi Khoury was promoted to Executive Vice President, Marketing & Digital Transformation.

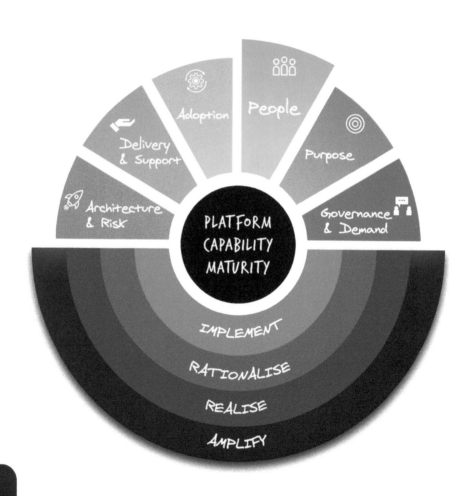

BECOMING MISSIONARIES

Sean, the Success Director for Jennifer's platform vendor, was in for his regular customer visit when he bumped into the company COO. The COO, Michael, was a personable type with a knack for remembering everybody's name.

'G'day Sean, haven't seen you around here for a while,' he remarked.

'Hi Michael, good to see you. I'm actually here to tell Jennifer some exciting news,' Sean replied with an enthusiastic grin.

'Oh yeah, what's that?' inquired Michael.

'Jennifer's team recently created some seriously innovative customisations to our platform that our engineers have said are not only groundbreaking, but they didn't believe possible. Her lead developer showcased it to our chief engineer in San Fran last night, and the message has gone global. There are some serious heavy hitters in our organisation taking notice and entire teams of engineers across the globe asking me to set up meetings with your team to unpack how they achieved it.'

'We do like to push the boundaries around here, Sean,' Michael quipped, 'I'm always glad to hear when our people are doing well. Just make sure your guys don't distract the team, and I'll be sure to congratulate Jennifer when I see her next. Anyway, thanks, Sean, good to see you. I better keep moving,' and with that, Michael was on his way.

TRIBE OF MENTORS

Imagine your organisation's potential to scale and innovate if all employees across the business performed at the same level of maturity and the best talent in the market wanted to join you on that journey? How might we achieve this?

Perhaps the most significant mechanism to achieve amplification of value across the organisation is achieved by creating high performing capabilities around all of your platforms.

To achieve this, we amplify the power of your people by creating a tribe of mentors.

WHY MENTORING?

A digital transformation requires thinking big. Incremental advancements are not sufficient in the face of constant disruption. It's not enough to be able to make short-term wins in what Simon Sinek would describe as 'the infinite game'. The organisation must continually evolve to meet the changing needs of customers.

> To sustain growth and innovation in the face of disruption, your platform team's human and process capabilities need to be amplified via mentoring across and outside the organisation.

To sustain growth and innovation in the face of disruption, your platform team's human and process capabilities need to be amplified via mentoring across and outside the organisation.

All that said, a full agile transformation might be a huge stretch because changing organisational mindset at scale is difficult. This is why I believe adopting a formalised mentoring approach is so important to amplifying value.

Research by Gartner in 2006 found retention rates for mentees was 72 per cent compared to 49 per cent for non-participants. Mentorship has also shown to have a significant positive impact on diversity. Cornell University found its mentorship programs increased diversity in management by up to 34 per cent and promotion rates by up to 38 per cent (Beheshti, 2019).

So how do we move our platform capability from masters to missionaries? Here's a diagram I often use to describe the journey.

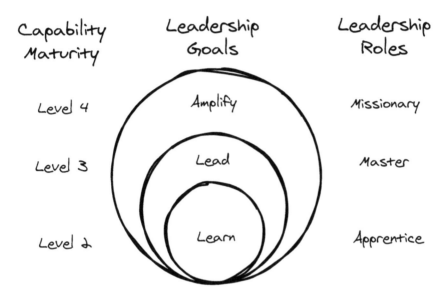

Capability Maturity	Leadership Goals	Leadership Roles
Level 4	Amplify	Missionary
Level 3	Lead	Master
Level 2	Learn	Apprentice

INTRINSIC AMPLIFICATION: MENTORING THROUGH GUILDS

If you've ever looked into scaled Agile or have been pitched an agile transformation or training, you might have heard about The Spotify Model or terms such as Tribes, Chapters, Guilds, and Squads. Guilds have been evangelised by many prominent names in technology, like Spotify, to promote excellence in a particular capability and keep agile teams from siloing.

Guilds are, in essence, groups of people who work in separate teams on different products, systems or platforms and report to different managers but perform a similar function. With the leader's help, they come together to set a shared vision, mission, and strategy for their

> To be successful, this cannot be ad hoc. Research suggests that poor mentoring is more detrimental than no mentoring.

craft and then support each other to lift the maturity of this capability across all the teams.

To be successful, this cannot be ad hoc. Research suggests that poor mentoring is more detrimental than no mentoring (Scandura, 1998). Therefore this process should be formalised with guilds led by capable mentors. A great non-technology example of this in practice is the John Hopkins School of Medicine, which, in 2012, made mentoring selection a competitive process with benefits and rewards, which proved to significantly increase the results of their mentoring program (Johnson, et al., 2020).

Just as religious missionaries explored the far corners of the world to bring enlightenment to all people, the goal of your capability mentors is to establish guilds and standardise and lift capability across the organisation. Having your leads take on the foundational leadership roles for their appropriate guilds is a practical, feasible, and impactful way to amplify your platform team's value.

EXTRINSIC AMPLIFICATION: GIVING BACK

At Level Three, we discussed the importance of leveraging our networks. It's now time to focus the value of our capability outward from the organisation, give back to our networks and in turn amplify the value of our brand and our employee value proposition.

While I'm sure you could immediately think of many ways to achieve this, I have seen four that work particularly well in a mature capability team.

1. Speaking at industry conferences. Sharing the capabilities journey successes and learnings from the platform is a great way to keep your team engaged, reflect on their value, and build the team's brand in the community.

2. Publish a blog. For the introverts who are perhaps intimidated by the prospect of public speaking, contributing to a public blog is an excellent way to share your story. Obviously, this would focus on non-commercially sensitive projects and highlight the safe learning culture you have developed.

3. Opensource your code. Ask your team to publicly publish their code for other external developers and teams to see. As with the blog or speaking engagements, publish nothing commercially sensitive or that weakens your competitive advantage. However, publishing code for external review is a great way to make sure your team are writing quality software (public peer review can be confronting and rewarding) and demonstrating the unique culture you have cultivated. Contributing code to the community also has the benefit that external developers can enhance the software, and you may choose to utilise this freely contributed enhancement into your environment or hire that person into your team.

4. Host industry events. Platform user groups are always looking for hosts. Typically the platform vendor will sponsor some of the publicly organised user group events as a way of giving back. You, too, can contribute by hosting an event. Use this opportunity to have your team practice speaking with a friendly audience, showcase your team and work, and start conversations with attendees to seek out potential new employees.

PEOPLE

MEASURING THE RETURN

We've already covered various case studies and research about the value of mentoring in terms of retention and diversity in management, but let's not ignore the importance of unlocking the scale and innovation that comes from unified leadership and process approaches across the organisation.

Internal return aside, it is also worth noting the value of external amplification. Ben Duncombe, a Salesforce specialist recruiter in Sydney, Australia, noted that employer brand is often an influencing factor in his ability to source top talent for clients. In episode five (01 April 2021) of my *Platform Diaries* podcast, Ben recalled approaching a highly sought after candidate who had no interest in changing roles. But upon mentioning the name of the employer, the candidate became immediately interested and was ultimately recruited. This candidate was aware of the company and familiar with the platform owner and work of the team through their blog and industry conference keynotes. The candidate was a prize catch attracted not by the technology or the money but the opportunity to be involved in a platform team with such a strong public brand and employee value proposition.

> The candidate was a prize catch attracted not by the technology or the money but the opportunity to be involved in a platform team with such a strong public brand and employee value proposition.

Jennifer was standing backstage with her lead consultant Diego as some fifteen hundred keen engineers and interested customers filled the auditorium at the conference centre in downtown San Francisco.

'I've never spoken to a group this large before,' whispered Jennifer nervously to her counterpart, hoping the lapel microphone wouldn't pick it up.

'What?' Diego gasped loudly. 'Six months ago, I'd never spoken in public at all, and now I'm standing next to you about to go out there, and you tell me this is your first rodeo?' 'It's all good; we've got this,' Jennifer said assertively, hoping to reassure herself as much as Diego.

The innovation that Jennifer's team had delivered had blown the minds of the vendor's engineers so significantly that Jennifer was asked to travel to their global conference to showcase the work. Their presentation went off without a hitch, and afterwards, a line of fifty excited engineers waited to ask Diego how to get access to the software and how to apply for roles in Jennifer's team. Meanwhile, a journalist from the premier technology news website interviewed Jennifer, and published several articles about their work, team culture, and ways of working.

Shortly after returning home, Sean, their vendor's success director, presented the team with an innovation award and Jennifer was approached by a VC funded fintech startup to join as their CTO.

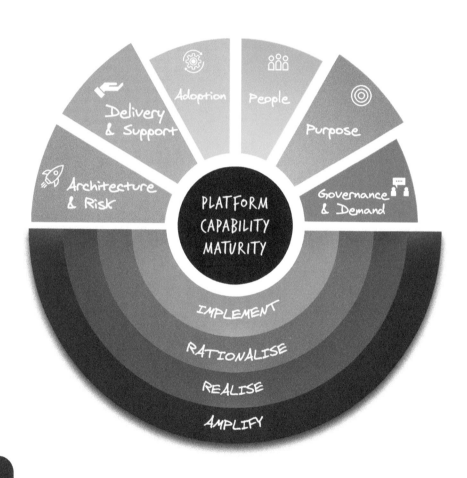

DO THE RIGHT THING

'I suppose it is tempting, if the only tool you have is a hammer, to treat everything as if it were a nail.'
– Abraham H Maslow.

THE VALUE TRAP

When attempting to take an organisation-wide view to amplify value, unconscious bias can kick in, and we tend to fall into the value trap. It is a false assumption that using a single platform for everything reduces complexity and enables the realisation of scale and innovation. It's also understandable that we, as seasoned platform owners, fall into this trap.

> When attempting to take an organisation-wide view to amplify value, unconscious bias can kick in, and we tend to fall into the value trap.

1. For a long time, you've been advocating for your platform. The assumption being that the more strategically important the platform, the more powerful you become.

2. Vendors perpetuate this message because by convincing you to bring more capabilities onto their platform under the guise of simplification or some other aspirational value measure, they ensure more of your software dollars come their way. After all, it's their job to sell you more software.

3. Senior leaders see the success of your capability, and because they don't see value in their platform, they ask if yours can solve

their problems, reinforcing the message that your platform is the only valuable one.

DON'T GET CAUGHT

Hopefully, you know why this is a problem. That's right – value comes from building the capability around the platform, not building monoliths.

Remember way back at Level One when we first discussed adoption? One of the core principles was building something that people want to use – something that makes their lives easier. That won't be easy if we aren't using the right tool for the job. As Zubair Ahmed, SVP, Head of IT & Business Innovation, Emirates Islamic Bank, said, 'let the innovation efforts be targeted towards the need and not the technology' (Ahmed, n.d.).

Understanding the various domains and selecting the right tool for the job makes a lot more sense. So rather than treating our platform like a Birmingham screwdriver, we can seek to identify the best tools for the various jobs and then strategically solve the value equation.

CONSUME OR CONSECRATE

When working with platform leaders on this topic, our challenge is often to understand how to objectively identify where and when to use their platform. To help guide their thinking, I offer these four simple principles:

1. Know your sweet spot
2. Target the right domains
3. Be a good supplier to the others
4. Think broadly and do the right thing.

The philosophy behind these principles is to amplify value by focusing transformation effort on recognising and leveraging platform specialisation. In simple terms, it's about identifying the right tool for the job and getting maximum value from each tool.

To help with that identification process, I came up with this simple model.

> In simple terms, it's about identifying the right tool for the job and getting maximum value from each tool.

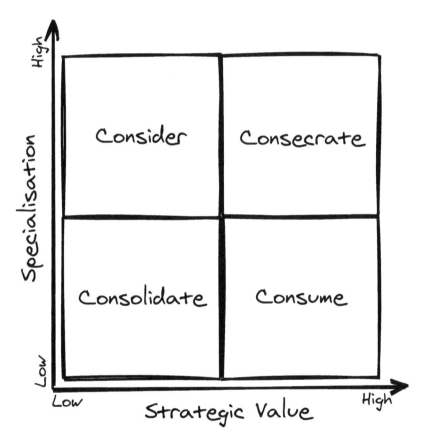

The left side of the decision matrix describes solutions with limited strategic value. Where these are highly specialised, it might make

> Low specialisation and low strategic value mean there is limited value in bringing them onto the strategic platforms, and a better approach would be to retire as many as possible.

sense to simply keep an eye on them for future opportunities but do nothing for now. Low specialisation and low strategic value mean there is limited value in bringing them onto the strategic platforms, and a better approach would be to retire as many as possible.

At the right of the model is where we focus our energy and deploy what Paul Willmott, director at McKinsey London, describes as 'plug and play dynamics' (Willmott, 2014). This is the process of attacking specific areas of the value chain without owning the whole thing.

As the platform owner who understands the sweet spot for your platform, you have a couple of options to consider.

1. Consume: Where it makes sense, amplify the value your platform brings to the organisation by strategically bringing together more business functions and capabilities and retiring redundant platforms.

2. Consecrate: Where a particular platform is objectively the best tool for the job, then your platform team should be amplifying value for the organisation by being a good supplier and ensuring the timely and accurate flow of data to and from the platform needing it; ultimately increasing the maturity of that platform.

The lesson here is that to amplify value, we need to look objectively at platforms and take the sensible view of 'company first' rather than 'platform first'. Know your sweet spot, think broadly and do the right thing.

I recently worked with a platform owner from a digital advertising business with a very mature CRM platform implementation. The business had been investing heavily in digital customer products but had experienced three consecutive quarters of negative growth, which resulted in downsizing.

Using this model, we identified that politics over which tool to use for the job resulted in a bottleneck. A lack of resources focused on unlocking value from the CRM platform and subsequently a proliferation of point solutions and compounding technical debt accrued because the platform team was unable to amplify their value by being a good supplier.

When the platform owner and product teams agreed on the organisation's domain model, resources were allocated across the portfolio to unlock the value, and new product innovation velocity was restored. The fiscal recovery was underway.

FINAL THOUGHTS

So there you have it, the Platform Maturity Journey.

How are you feeling?

Did you volunteer for the role, or have you fallen into it?

Have you worked out what level of maturity your capability is at today and where you think you want to get to?

Do you know who should be your executive sponsor/stakeholder, and do they have your back?

What is your 'why' and how does it align with the platform and organisational 'why'?

What is ahead of you to truly get adoption from your stakeholders?

What is your employee value proposition? Have you considered why people would want to work in your team?

Is your team psychologically safe, and will they constructively challenge each other?

Do you have a plan for managing scope and ruthless prioritisation?

How will you leverage your knowledge, network and partners to bring innovation to the organisation?

Is your team on the path to becoming a tribe of mentors?

Can you see yourself on the big stage at a vendor keynote in some foreign land, or right now, would you just be happy to know how to take the first step?

How will you amplify value in your organisation?

My aim was to provide a guidebook to help you answer these questions along with some useful models and stories – all to encourage you to consider how you will solve these problems, your way, in your organisational context.

Every organisation has different history, market, technology and people, and that's why I love working with people like you to navigate your platform journey. I've had the support of some fine mentors throughout my career, and now, if you'd like my help, I'd love to be yours.

Please reach out, share your story with me and tell me what you think about the book. I'd love to have a conversation about your journey.

REFERENCES

Ahmed, Z., n.d. *Innovation - Should it be technology or business led?*.
[Online]
Available at: https://www.cxoconnectme.com/innovation/
innovation--should-it-be-technology-or-business-led/
[Accessed March 2021].

Andreasson, I., 2010. How to avoid throwing innovation out with the
wastewater. *Lean Magazine*, September, pp. 15-18.

Andreasson, I., 2011. Getting flow into your product development.
Lean Magazine, Issue 6,8.

Armandpour, T., 2017. *Owning Your Code is Better*. [Online]
Available at: https://www.pagerduty.com/blog/developers-own-
code/).
[Accessed March 2021].

Baird, N., 2020. *Innovator's Playbook: How to Create Great Products,
Services and Experiences That Your Customers Will Love*. Milton,
Qld: John Wiley & Sons Australia.

Beheshti, N., 2019. *Improve Workplace Culture With A Strong
Mentoring Program*. [Online]
Available at: https://www.forbes.com/sites/
nazbeheshti/2019/01/23/improve-workplace-culture-with-a-
strong-mentoring-program/?sh=464b9f9776b5
[Accessed March 2021].

Crozier, R., 2018. *REA Group finds 'ludicrous mode' for Salesforce development.* [Online]
Available at: https://www.itnews.com.au/news/rea-group-finds-ludicrous-mode-for-salesforce-development-514165
[Accessed March 2021].

Crozier, R., 2019. *Telstra expands its use of Salesforce.* [Online]
Available at: https://www.itnews.com.au/news/telstra-expands-it's-use-of-salesforce-529673
[Accessed March 2021].

Duhigg, C., 2016. *What Google Learned From Its Quest to Build the Perfect Team.* [Online]
Available at: https://www.nytimes.com/2016/02/28/magazine/what-google-learned-from-its-quest-to-build-the-perfect-team.html
[Accessed March 2021].

Edmondson, A. C., 2018. *The Fearless Organization: Creating Psychological Safety in the Workplace for Learning, Innovation, and Growth.* Hoboken, New Jersey: John Wiley & Sons.

Galetti, B., 2020. *How Amazon is built to try and learn.* [Online]
Available at: https://www.mckinsey.com/business-functions/mckinsey-digital/our-insights/fasttimes/interviews/beth-galetti
[Accessed March 2021].

Gavin, R. et al., 2020. *The B2B digital inflection point: How sales have changed during COVID-19.* [Online]
Available at: https://www.mckinsey.com/business-functions/marketing-and-sales/our-insights/the-b2b-digital-inflection-point-how-sales-have-changed-during-covid-19
[Accessed March 2021].

Gilligan's Island. 1964-1967. [Film] Directed by Sherwood Schwartz. USA: A Gladasya - United Artists Television Production.

Groysberg, B., Lee, J., Price, J. & Cheng, &. J. Y.-J., 2018. *The Leader's Guide to Corporate Culture.* [Online]
Available at: https://hbr.org/2018/01/the-leaders-guide-to-corporate-culture
[Accessed March 2021].

Haenfler, R., 2013. *Subcultures: The Basics.* e-book ed. London: Routledge.

Hirshberg, J., 1998. *The Creative Priority - Putting Innovation To Work In Your Business.* New York: HarperBusiness.

Hubbard, D., 2014. *How to Measure Anything : Finding the value of intangibles in business.* 3rd ed. New York: John Wiley & Sons.

Johnson, W. B., Smith, D. G. & Haythornthwaite, J., 2020. *Why Your Mentorship Program Isn't Working.* [Online]
Available at: https://hbr.org/2020/07/why-your-mentorship-program-isnt-working
[Accessed March 2021].

Jolly, R., 2011. *The Paradox of Indispensibility.* [Online]
Available at: https://onlinelibrary.wiley.com/doi/epdf/10.1111/j.1467-8616.2011.00771.x
[Accessed March 2021].

Knesek, D., 2016. *Averting a "Technical Debt" Crisis (Part 1).* [Online]
Available at: https://www.linkedin.com/pulse/averting-technical-debt-crisis-part-1-doug-knesek/
[Accessed March 2021].

Madhani, P., 2017. Six Sigma Deployment in Sales and Marketing: Enhancing Competitive Advantages. *The IUP Journal of Business Strategy,* XIV(No 2).

Marr, B., 2016. *Are These The 7 Real Reasons Why Tech Projects Fail?.* [Online]
Available at: https://www.forbes.com/sites/bernardmarr/2016/09/13/are-these-the-real-reasons-why-tech-projects-fail/?sh=79a7352l7320)
[Accessed March 2021].

Maurya, A., 2016. *Scaling Lean: Mastering the key metrics for startup growth.* New York: Penguin Random House.

McKinsey & Company, 2020. *The Next Normal: The recovery will be digital..* [Online]
Available at: https://www.mckinsey.com/~/media/McKinsey/Business%20Functions/McKinsey%20Digital/Our%20Insights/How%20six%20companies%20are%20using%20technology%20and%20data%20to%20transform%20themselves/The-next-normal-the-recovery-will-be-digital.pdf
[Accessed 2021].

Mitchell, R. A. B. a. W. D., 1997. Toward a Theory of Stakeholder Identification and Salience: Defining the Principle of Who and What Really Counts. *Academy of Management Review,* 22 (https://doi.org/10.5465/amr.1997.9711022105), p. 853–886.

Onno Boer, S. C. M. S. &. A. T., 2018. *Zero-based productivity—Organization: Using zero-based principles to forge a purpose-built organization.* [Online]
Available at: https://www.mckinsey.com/business-functions/operations/our-insights/zero-based-productivity-organization-using-zero-based-principles-to-forge-a-purpose-built-

organization
[Accessed March 2021].

Project Management Institute, 2017. *Pulse of the Profession 2017: 9th Global Project Management Survey.* [Online]
Available at: https://www.pmi.org/-/media/pmi/documents/
public/pdf/learning/thought-leadership/pulse/pulse-of-the-
profession-2017.pdf
[Accessed March 2021].

Radigan, D., n.d. *Escaping the black hole of technical debt.* [Online]
Available at: https://www.atlassian.com/agile/software-
development/technical-debt
[Accessed March 2021].

Rajesh Solanki, O. P. Y. &. B. N., 2011. Improving the NPD Process
by Applying Lean Principles: A Case Study. *Engineering
Management Journal,* Vol 23 (No 1).

Reichheld, F. F., 2003. *The One Number You Need to Grow.* [Online]
Available at: https://hbr.org/2003/12/the-one-number-you-need-
to-grow
[Accessed 2021].

Reinertsen, D. G., 2009. *The Principles of Product Development Flow:
Second generation lean product development.* Redondo Beach,
CA: Celeritas Publishing.

Romanowski, P., George-Warren, H. & Pareles, J., 2001. *The Rolling
Stone Encyclopedia of Rock and Roll.* London: Fireside Books.

Romero, T., 2002. *All it takes is a bit of inspired teamwork.* [Online]
[Accessed March 2021].

Salesforce, 2021. *Customer success stories.* [Online]
Available at: https://www.salesforce.com/au/customer-success-

stories/telstra/
[Accessed MArch 2021].

Scandura, T. A., 1998. Dysfunctional Mentoring Relationships and
Outcomes. *Journal of Management,* 2, Issue 4(https://journals.
sagepub.com/doi/10.1177/014920639802400307), pp. 449-467.

Sinek, S., 2011. *Start with Why.* Harlow, England: Penguin Books.

Stephen R. Covey, B. E. &. B. W., 2009. *Predictable Results in
Unpredictable Times.* Salt Lake City, Utah: Franklin Covey.

The Butterfly Effect. 2004. [Film] Directed by J. Mackye Gruber Eric
Bress. Canada: BenderSpink, FilmEngine.

Trice, H. M., 1993. *Occupational Subcultures in the Workplace.* Ithaca,
N.Y.: ILR Press.

Voisey, J., Baty, D. & Delany, K., 2002. *PWC Global Human Capital
Survey 2002.* [Online]
Available at: www.factline.com/fsDownload/ger_150_Report-exec-
briefing.pdf?forumid=183&v=1&id=117300
[Accessed March 2021].

Walker, B. H. &. D., 2016. The enormous cost of IT project failure. *In
The Black,* 01 November.

Walsh, J., 2014. *Vladimir Putin employs a full-time food taster to
ensure his meals aren't poisoned.* [Online]
Available at: https://www.independent.co.uk/news/world/europe/
vladimir-putin-employs-full-time-food-taster-ensure-his-meals-
aren-t-poisoned-9624380.html
[Accessed March 2021].

Williams, S., 2021. *Platform Diaries,* Melbourne: s.n.

Willink, J., 2018. *Extreme Ownership*. s.l.:MacMillan Australia.

Willmott, P., 2014. *Digital strategy*. [Online]
Available at: https://www.mckinsey.com/business-functions/
mckinsey-digital/our-insights/digital-strategy
[Accessed March 2021].

Zoominfo, n.d. *NewsXtend*. [Online]
Available at: https://www.zoominfo.com/c/news-xtend/372295996
[Accessed March 2021].

ABOUT THE AUTHOR

Shane Williams has always been fascinated by the next exciting tech – it drove his parents crazy. He loved his Commodore 64, not just for the games, but so he could pull it apart to see how it worked (and sometimes put it back together). In an ironic twist, one of Shane's three sons has the same interest.

The Platform Owner's Guidebook is the book Shane wished he'd had when he started trying to build platforms that delivered value to their owners and users. He has a total aversion to organisations handing out money on the basis of vague promises, or spending money for minimal return.

As an executive tech expert, Shane works with digital native businesses that are expanding into adjacent or global markets. He helps businesses that choose or are forced to change, as he understands what it takes to make technology successful at scale. His corporate clients recognise Shane as their go-to person for sound, independent, practical advice that transforms their businesses.

When not in front of a client or a screen, Shane can be found riding motorbikes or camping out in the bush with his kids.

To find out how Shane can help you and your organisation, visit:

www.shanewillams.com.au